Better Homes and Gardens®

WOOD™
WEEKEND TOY PROJECTS
YOU CAN MAKE

WE CARE!

All of us at Meredith® Books are dedicated to giving you the
information and ideas you need to create beautiful and useful
woodworking projects. We guarantee your satisfaction with this
book for as long as you own it. We also welcome your comments
and suggestions. Please write us at Meredith® Books, BB-117,
1716 Locust St., Des Moines, IA 50309-3023.

A **WOOD**™ **BOOK**
Published by Meredith® Books

MEREDITH® **BOOKS**
President, Book Group: Joseph J. Ward
Vice President and Editorial Director: Elizabeth P. Rice
Executive Editor: Connie Schrader
Art Director: Ernest Shelton
Prepress Production Manager: Randall Yontz

WOOD® MAGAZINE
President, Magazine Group: William T. Kerr
Editor: Larry Clayton

WEEKEND TOY PROJECTS YOU CAN MAKE
Produced by Roundtable Press, Inc.
Directors: Susan E. Meyer, Marsha Melnick
Senior Editor: Marisa Bulzone
Managing Editor: Ross L. Horowitz
Graphic Designer: Leah Lococo
Design Assistant: Leslie Goldman
Art Assistant: Ahmad Mallah
Copy Assistant: Amy Handy

For Meredith® **Books**
Editorial Project Manager/Assistant Art Director: Tom Wegner
Contributing How-To Editors: Marlen Kemmet,
    Charles E. Sommers
Contributing Techniques Editor: Bill Krier
Contributing Tool Editor: Larry Johnston
Contributing Outline Editor: David A. Kirchner

Special thanks to Khristy Benoit

On the front cover: Rough 'N' Ready Wrecker, pages 36–39
On the back cover: Fashion-Doll Armoire, pages 90-95 (left);
    Giddyap Rocking Horse, pages 26–29 (top right);
    Sea Skipper for Young Fliers, pages 64–65 (bottom right)

CREATURES FROM THE ANIMAL KINGDOM

A miniature menagerie awaits you here, from a captivating caterpillar puzzle and a dazzling dinosaur, to a rock 'n' rolling worm waiting to wiggle its way into any child's heart.

PUZZLED PUSSYCAT

Cat fanciers and children will be clawing at you to build this project. Our pattern, complete with its painting guide, will make finishing as simple as painting by number.

First, saw the cat to shape

1. Sand both sides of your 1½×8×13" piece of pine (we started with a 2×10) with 80- and 150-grit sandpapers. If you don't have stock this wide, you can laminate two pieces of ¾"-thick material to make up the blank.

2. Make a copy of the full-sized cat pattern found on *pages 6–7*, and apply it to one face of the piece. (We photocopied the pattern, and then adhered it to the pine with spray adhesive.)

3. Using a ⅛" bandsaw blade or 2mm skip-tooth scrollsaw blade, saw around the perimeter of the cat's body (Line 1 on the pattern), start at the outside ear and then work around the cat's back, tail, and paws. (We cut just outside of the pattern line and then sanded to the line using our disc and drum sanders. We also found that over-tensioning the scrollsaw blade slightly produced a smoother cut in this thicker stock.) Saw the five paw lines.

4. In scrap, bore a ⅝" hole and test the fit of your cat-eye marbles; they should fit snugly. (We found marbles vary in size so adjust the hole diameter to fit your marbles.) Now, bore the eye sockets and the ¾" hole in the center of letter A. (We used Forstner bits and backed the piece to prevent chip-out when drilling these holes.)

5. Cut away the cat's head by following Line 2. (If you're using a bandsaw, switch to a ⅛" blade for this and all remaining cuts. For the inside cuts, we cut on the line.) Next, starting at the tail, saw along Line 3, cut around letter C, and remove it. Next, cut out letter A and then T, sawing in the direction indicated by the arrows. Now, make the last sawcut along Line 6 so you can separate the upper and lower parts.

6. Hand-sand a slight round-over on all edges. To help with painting, score along the stripes and face details with an X-acto knife. Now, remove the paper pattern. (We used lacquer thinner to remove the adhesive residue.)

Here comes the fun: Personalizing your cat

Note: We suggest using acrylic paints. You'll find brands such as Accent, Apple Barrel, Folk Art, and Liquitex available at most well-stocked crafts stores. Follow our color scheme for the cat and the letters, or select you own colors. We recommend applying the paints with a number 5 red sable or similar brush.

1. Brush on the first coat of golden brown over entire cat body and head, but do not paint the muzzle, paws, or tip of the tail. Allow this paint to dry thoroughly before applying a second coat.

2. While the paint on the cat body parts dries, paint the CAT letters burgundy. Also, paint the cat's muzzle, tail tip, and paws antique white or light tan.

3. Paint the brown stripes. (We used burnt sienna.) For a three-dimensional effect, paint stripes across the edges and back of the cat, too. While the body stripes dry, add the brown ears and stripes to all sides of the cat's face.

4. For the inside of the ears and the nose, apply a coat of light magenta. After that dries, accent the area by diluting red to create a dark pink. Paint the tongue red.

5. Outline the eye area and inside the ⅝" holes with yellow paint. Add freckles (dots for whiskers) and toe lines by applying dark brown paint where indicated.

6. If you'd like, outline the ears, eyes, mouth, muzzle, nose, and paws with a black permanent marker. (We had excellent results using a Sanford extra-fine-point Sharpie marker, available at office-supply and art-supply stores.)

7. After the paint has dried thoroughly, brush or spray on a sealing coat of polyurethane.

8. Press the marbles into the eye sockets (two on each side). If young children will be playing with this puzzle, epoxy the marbles in the eye sockets so they can't be removed or fall out accidentally.

Project Tool List
Tablesaw
Bandsaw or scrollsaw
Disc sander
Drill press
   Sanding drum
   Bits: ⅝", ¾"
Finishing sander

Note: We built the project using the tools listed. You may be able to substitute other tools or equipment for listed items you don't have. Additional common tools and clamps may be required to complete the project.

continued

PUZZLED PUSSYCAT
continued

FULL-SIZED PATTERN

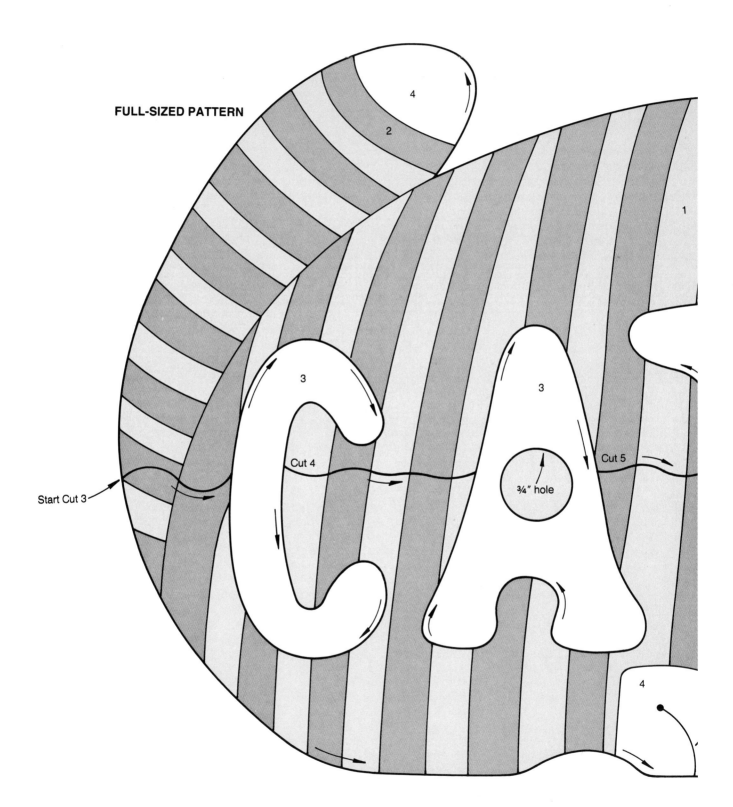

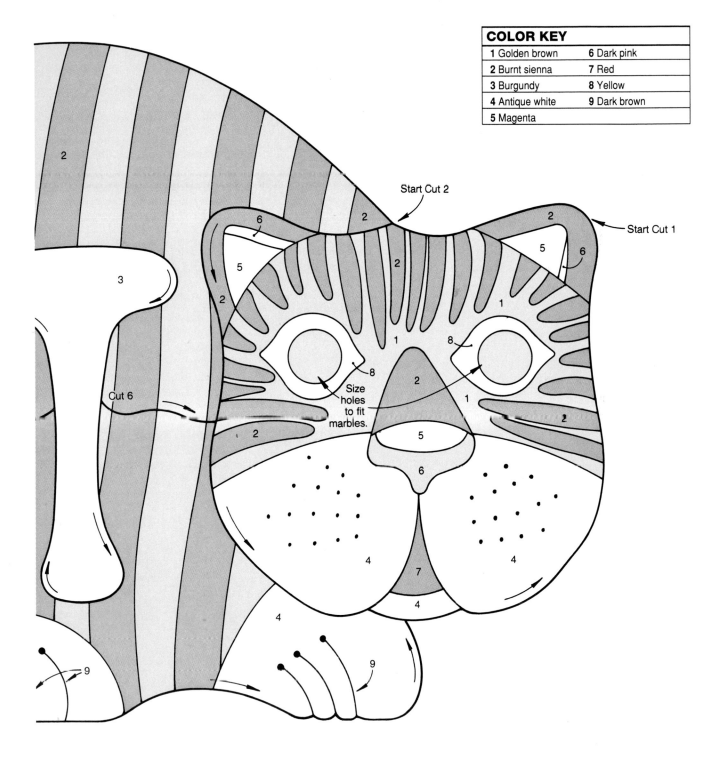

COLOR KEY

1 Golden brown		**6** Dark pink	
2 Burnt sienna		**7** Red	
3 Burgundy		**8** Yellow	
4 Antique white		**9** Dark brown	
5 Magenta			

Start Cut 2

Start Cut 1

Cut 6

Size holes to fit marbles.

KING OF THE CATERPILLARS

fast enough that you don't scorch the wood beside the line. Lift the pen from the wood periodically to let the tip reheat.

4. Sand all surfaces smooth, removing traces of pattern lines that remain. (We also sanded away a few scorch marks.) Now, add some accents with stains or acrylic artist's colors.

5. Paint the eyes solid white and black, but apply other colors as thinned washes. After the paint dries, coat both sides and all edges with clear, gloss polyurethane. Before you turn the caterpillar loose in the playroom, make sure the pieces slide together easily. If they don't, sand the mating edges with 220-grit sandpaper until they do, and touch up the gloss finish.

Project Tool List
  Scrollsaw or bandsaw
  Woodburning pen
  Finishing sander

  Note: *We built the project using the tools listed. You may be able to substitute other tools or equipment for listed items you don't have. Additional common tools and clamps may be required to complete the project.*

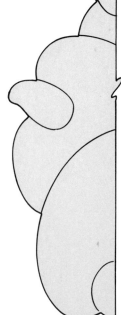

When it comes to entertainment, this king-sized caterpillar does double duty. A toddler will love fitting the big pieces together. And you'll have your fun, too, cutting those pieces, woodburning, and painting.

1. Trace the black cutting lines from the full-sized pattern onto a 1½x9¼x10" piece of stock (a 10" length of clear, straight-grained 2x10 fills the bill). Softwoods such as pine, fir, cedar, or redwood (our choice) work well.

2. Install a sharp blade in your scrollsaw (a good choice: Olson's no. 411 or similar, .110x.022" with 15 teeth per inch), and then scrollsaw around the outside line. Next, cut the inside lines to separate the four puzzle pieces. Sand slight round-overs along all of the edges.

3. Assemble the pieces, and trace the red woodburning lines onto your cutout. Burn the lines about ⅟₁₆" wide. Move the woodburning pen along the line at a steady speed—slowly enough to etch a solid, black line into the wood, but

HOP-ALONG GRASSHOPPER

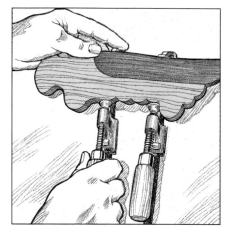

Cam-action rear wheels tell the tale of this friendly member from the insect world. Tug on the cord and our wooden grasshopper comes alive. Its hind legs—attached off-center on the rear wheels—give the illusion of propelling the bug forward, while causing the tail to bob up and down.

Make the body, wing, and leg parts first

1. Rip and crosscut one piece each of ¾"-thick mahogany and maple to 4½×12". (See the Cutting Diagram *opposite*.) Using double-faced tape, stick the pieces together, face to face.

2. Using carbon paper, transfer the full-sized Body and Wing pattern on *page 13* onto the face

of the maple piece. Mark the centerpoints for the two wheel axles, the leg axle, and the eye. With a drill press, drill the three ⁵⁄₁₆" holes and the ¼" eyehole through both pieces. (We backed all parts with scrap when drilling to prevent chip-out.)

3. Using a scrollsaw, follow the solid lines on the pattern, and saw the body and wing to shape. Separate the parts and remove the tape. Next, glue and clamp the mahogany wings (A) to the maple body (B) as shown *above right*. (We used yellow wood-worker's glue.) Remove the clamps after the glue dries. Sand all edges to remove any saw marks.

Note: *You can make a second grasshopper combining the remaining wing and body with the woods*

reversed. If you assemble the second one, you'll need to double the number of leg parts, axles, and wheels.

4. Trace two full-sized patterns (*page 13*) of the leg (C) onto a scrap piece of ¾"-thick mahogany. Mark the centerpoint for the ¼"-diameter hole on one face of each leg. Drill the ½"-deep holes in each piece. Next, scrollsaw the parts to shape. (If you prefer, stack the two pieces together to saw out both parts at once.) Using the pattern again, mark the screw pilot hole centerpoint on the face opposite the ¼" hole on each part. Drill these ³⁄₃₂" pilot holes ½" deep.

5. Resaw a ¾×2×6" piece of mahogany to ¼" thick. (We used our tablesaw.) Sand both faces on the piece. Trace two copies of the rearleg pattern (D) onto the face of the piece. Mark the center-points for the ⅛" screw holes. Drill the four holes. Scrollsaw the parts to shape.

6. Crosscut a 2¼"-long piece of 1"-diameter birch dowel for the pull string's knob. Sand the sharp edges to round them over. Clamp the knob in a wood-screw clamp and drill a ⅛" hole through the dowel at the center for the pull string.

continued

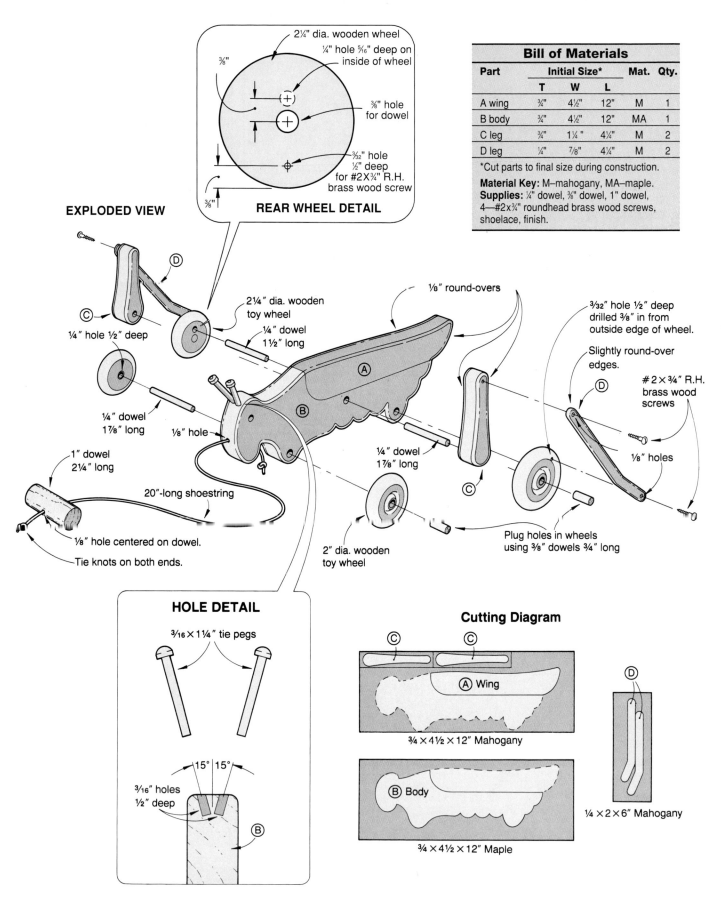

REAR WHEEL DETAIL

2¼" dia. wooden wheel

¼" hole ⁵⁄₁₆" deep on inside of wheel

⅜"

⅜" hole for dowel

³⁄₃₂" hole ½" deep for #2X¾" R.H. brass wood screw

⅜"

Bill of Materials

Part	Initial Size*			Mat.	Qty.
	T	W	L		
A wing	¾"	4½"	12"	M	1
B body	¾"	4½"	12"	MA	1
C leg	¾"	1¼"	4¼"	M	2
D leg	¼"	⅞"	4¼"	M	2

*Cut parts to final size during construction.

Material Key: M–mahogany, MA–maple.
Supplies: ¼" dowel, ⅜" dowel, 1" dowel, 4—#2x¾" roundhead brass wood screws, shoelace, finish.

EXPLODED VIEW

2¼" dia. wooden toy wheel

¼" dowel 1½" long

⅛" round-overs

³⁄₃₂" hole ½" deep drilled ⅜" in from outside edge of wheel.

Slightly round-over edges.

#2 × ¾" R.H. brass wood screws

¼" hole ½" deep

¼" dowel 1⅞" long

⅛" hole

1" dowel 2¼" long

⅛" holes

20"-long shoestring

¼" dowel 1⅞" long

⅛" hole centered on dowel.

Tie knots on both ends.

2" dia. wooden toy wheel

Plug holes in wheels using ⅜" dowels ¾" long

HOLE DETAIL

³⁄₁₆ × 1¼" tie pegs

15° 15°

³⁄₁₆" holes ½" deep

Cutting Diagram

Ⓒ Ⓒ

Ⓐ Wing

¾ × 4½ × 12" Mahogany

Ⓑ Body

¾ × 4½ × 12" Maple

Ⓓ

¼ × 2 × 6" Mahogany

11

HOP-ALONG GRASSHOPPER
continued

7. Chuck a ¼" round-over bit in your router, and round over the edges on the body. (As shown *below,* we placed the grasshopper's body on a ½"-thick foam pad while routing the edges.)

8. Finish-sand all parts. Hand-sand a slight round-over on the edges of leg parts C and D.

9. Crosscut four ¾" lengths of ⅜" dowel. Glue one in the hub of each wheel, aligning the dowels flush with the outside faces of the wheels. (See the Buying Guide *below right* for a source of ¾"-thick hardwood wheels.) Sand the dowels flush.

10. Using the dimensions on the Rear Wheel detail accompanying the Exploded View drawing on *page 11,* locate the centerpoint for ¼" off-centered axle holes on the inside of the rear wheels, and the screw pilot holes on the outside. Drill the ¼" axle holes ⁵⁄₁₆" deep and the ³⁄₃₂" pilot holes ½" deep. Next, locate the centerpoints on the inside of each front wheel and drill the ¼" holes ½" deep. (We made the scrap plywood jig shown *above right* to hold the wheels while drilling the axle holes.)

11. Cut two 1⅞" lengths and one 1½" length of ¼" dowel.

12. Trace the Face pattern *opposite* onto paper. Using the Body pattern as a guide, place the pattern on the front edge of the body's face area. Mark the centerpoints for the two angled antenna holes (see the Hole detail on the Exploded View drawing) and the hole for the pull cord. Drill the holes. (We clamped the body in a wood-screw clamp to hold it firmly, and then drilled the holes at the angle shown with a portable electric drill.)

Finish and assemble the grasshopper

1. Finish all parts before assembling. (We sprayed on three coats of glossy polyurethane and let each coat dry thoroughly. We sanded after the first two coats; rubbed the third coat with 0000 steel wool.)

2. Assemble the leg pairs as shown on the Exploded View drawing. Leave the screws slightly loose so the joints move freely.

3. Glue a 1⅞"-long axle dowel in the hub of one front wheel. Glue the second 1⅞"-long dowel in the ¼" hole of one leg part C. Glue the 1½"-long dowel in the off-centered axle hole in a rear wheel.

4. Place the front wheel axle through the front axle hole and glue on the opposite front wheel. (We allowed ⅛" of clearance between the wheels and body.) Next, insert the rear wheel axle through the rear hole, glue on the other rear wheel, and align them. Insert the dowel with leg part C attached to it, through the center hole in the body, glue on the other leg, and then align both legs. Finally, screw the leg parts D to the rear wheels.

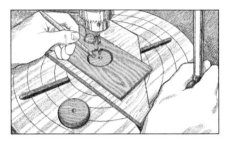

5. Thread the pull cord through the pull-knob and the hole in the grasshopper's nose and tie knots at each end. (We used a 20" length of shoelace.) Shorten the stem on the tie rack pegs (see the Buying Guide) to 1¼" long, and then glue one in each of the antenna holes.

Buying Guide
•**Grasshopper kit.** Catalog no. 3404. Kit includes enough wheels, pegs and dowel stock to make four toys. Contact Meisel Hardware Specialties for current price. Phone: 800-441-9870.

Project Tool List
Tablesaw
Scrollsaw
Drill
Drill press
   Bits: ³⁄₃₂", ⅛", ³⁄₁₆", ¼", ⁵⁄₁₆"
Router
   ¼" round-over bit
Finishing sander

Note: *We built the project using the tools listed. You may be able to substitute other tools or equipment for listed items you don't have. Additional common tools and clamps may be required to complete the project.*

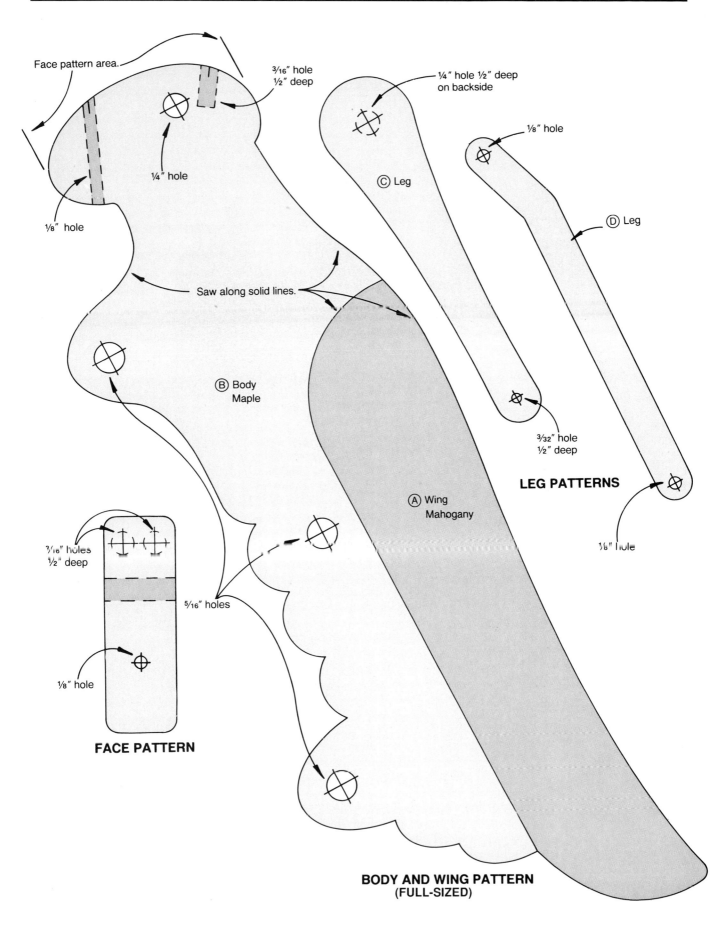

Face pattern area.

3/16" hole
1/2" deep

1/4" hole 1/2" deep
on backside

1/8" hole

Ⓒ Leg

Ⓓ Leg

1/4" hole

1/8" hole

Saw along solid lines.

Ⓑ Body
Maple

3/32" hole
1/2" deep

LEG PATTERNS

Ⓐ Wing
Mahogany

1/8" hole

3/16" holes
1/2" deep

5/16" holes

1/8" hole

FACE PATTERN

BODY AND WING PATTERN
(FULL-SIZED)

13

ROCK 'N' ROLL WIGGLE WORM

Once our small-fry learn to walk, they usually want someone to join them in their leisurely strolls through the living room and kitchen. Our tag-along wiggle worm promises hours of companionship and fun. On the roll, his segmented body rocks from side to side while his cam-driven antennae pump up and down.

Start with the body segments

1. Rip and crosscut two pieces of ¾" maple to 3½x20½". Face-join the two pieces to make a 1½"-thick lamination and clamp. After the glue dries, remove the clamps and plane or sand the bottom edge of the lamination flat. Now, crosscut it into four 5"-long rectangles.

2. Rip and crosscut two pieces of ¾" cherry to 3½x20½". Next, crosscut four 5"-long rectangles for the sides (A) from each piece.

3. Using carbon paper or a photocopier, make templates of the patterns on *page 17*. Mark the centerlines for the axle and the antennae holes on the A template. Now, cut it to shape with scissors.

4. Place the B template on one side of one maple rectangle, align the bottom and sides, and trace around the pattern's U-shape.

Do the same to the remaining maple rectangles. Bandsaw the U-shaped areas.

5. Form the body segments by gluing one cherry piece to each side of the U-shaped maple centers. Clamp all segments until the glue dries.

6. Scribe a centerline across the bottom of each body segment. Next, place the A template on the side of each segment, align at the bottom and the centerline, and trace around the curved template. Mark the centerpoints for the axles.

7. Bandsaw the body segments to shape. (We cut just outside the curved line, and then sanded to the line using our disc sander.) Next, select one of the segments for the head, center the A template on the side of it again, and using a try square, transfer the lines locating the antenna and eye holes across the sawn edge. Now, measure in 1" from each edge and mark antenna hole centerpoints.

8. Set up your table-mounted router as shown on the Chamfer detail on *page 16*. Chamfer the curved edges on both sides of all body segments. (We set the bit at ½" for the first pass, then reset it to ⅞" for the second pass.)

Next, drill the head, axles, and wheels

1. To drill the two angled holes for the antenna, chuck a ²¹⁄₆₄" bit in your drill press and tilt the table to 15° from horizontal. Next, rip a 12"-long, 7°-beveled shim from scrap and place it under the side edge of the head to be drilled to cant the head. See the Shim detail on *page 16*, and the Head detail *opposite*. Align the head and shim with the bit, clamp the head firmly, and then drill the hole as shown on *page 16, top*. Reposition the head and shim and drill the second hole.

2. Using the line you scribed across the head segment earlier, and the dimensions on the Head detail, plot the centerpoints for the two

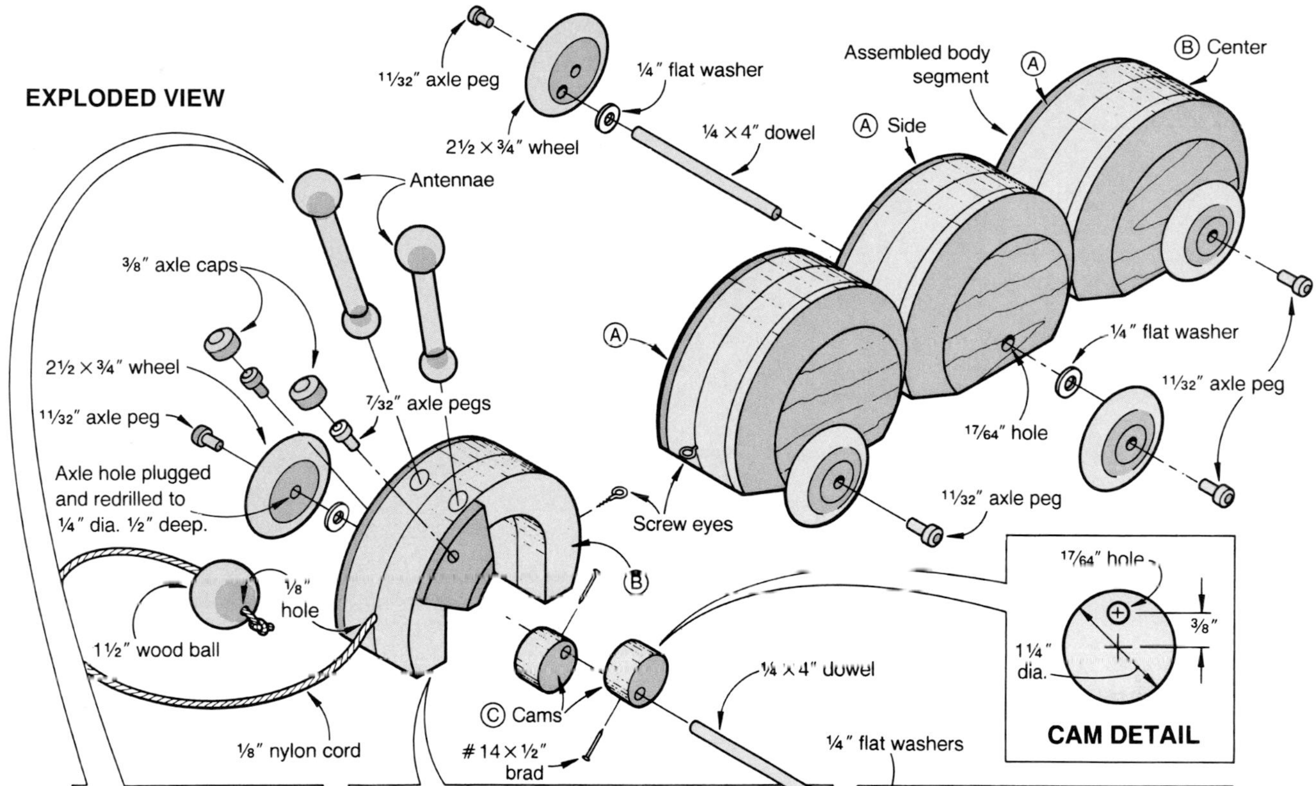
EXPLODED VIEW
11/32" axle peg
2½ × ¾" wheel
¼" flat washer
¼ × 4" dowel
Assembled body segment
Ⓐ
Ⓑ Center
Ⓐ Side
Antennae
⅜" axle caps
2½ × ¾" wheel
11/32" axle peg
7/32" axle pegs
Axle hole plugged and redrilled to ¼" dia. ½" deep.
⅛" hole
1½" wood ball
⅛" nylon cord
Ⓐ
Screw eyes
Ⓑ
Ⓒ Cams
#14 × ½" brad
¼ × 4" dowel
¼" flat washers
¼" flat washer
11/32" axle peg
17/64" hole
11/32" axle peg
17/64" hole
⅜"
1¼" dia.
CAM DETAIL

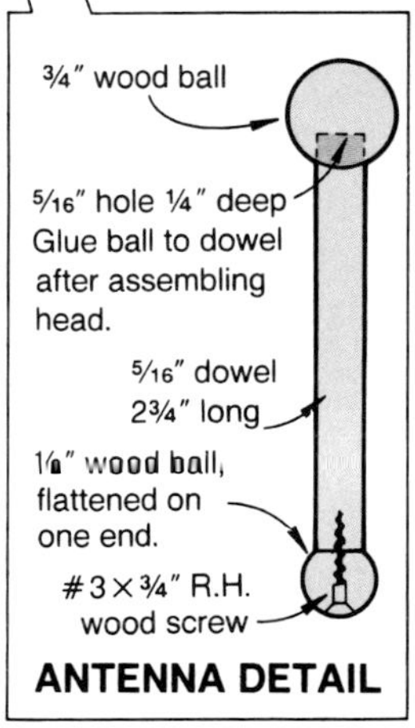
¾" wood ball
5/16" hole ¼" deep
Glue ball to dowel after assembling head.
5/16" dowel 2¾" long
½" wood ball, flattened on one end.
#3 × ¾" R.H. wood screw
ANTENNA DETAIL

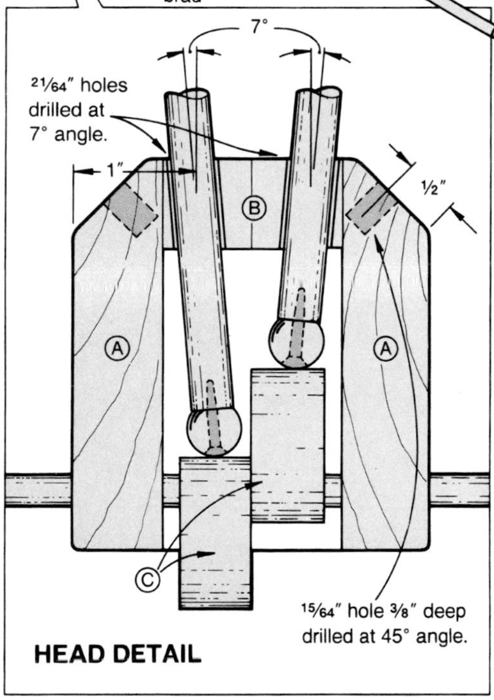
7°
21/64" holes drilled at 7° angle.
1"
½"
Ⓑ
Ⓐ
Ⓐ
Ⓒ
15/64" hole ⅜" deep drilled at 45° angle.
HEAD DETAIL

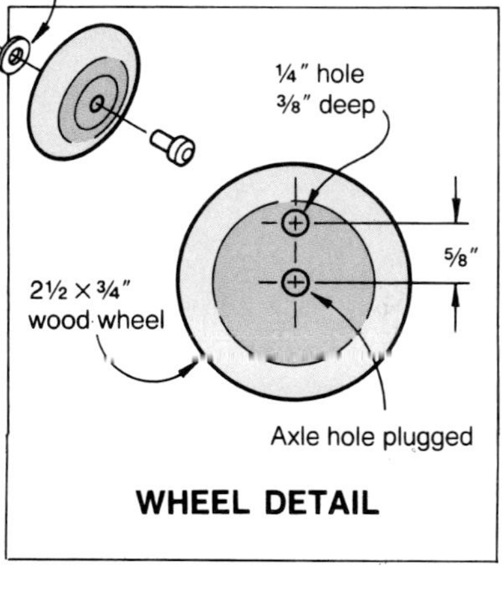
¼" hole ⅜" deep
⅝"
2½ × ¾" wood wheel
Axle hole plugged
WHEEL DETAIL

eyes. Switch to a 15/64" bit, tilt the drill press table to 45°, and align the bit with the centerpoint. Next, clamp the head in position, and then drill an eye hole. Now, drill the second eye hole. Change to a ⅛" bit and drill the hole for the pull cord.

3. Switch to a 17/64" bit and square the drill press table to the bit. Lay a body segment on its side on top of the piece of scrap, clamp, and drill an axle hole through the segment. Drill the axle holes in the other body segments the same way.

continued

Bill of Materials

Part	Finished Size*			Mat.	Qty.
	T	W	L		
A* side	¾"	3½"	5"	C	8
B* center	1½"	3½"	5"	M	4
C cam	1¼" dia.		11/16"	D	2

*Cut parts to final size during construction. Please read the instructions before cutting.

Material Key: C–cherry; M–maple; D–dowel
Supplies: ¼" dowel, 1¼" dowel, 5/16" dowel, axle pegs, axle caps, 8—¼" flat washers, 1½" wooden ball, ½" wooden balls, ¾" wooden balls, screw eyes, 2—#3X¾" roundhead wood screws, 2—#14X½" brads, nylon pull cord.

ROCK 'N' ROLL WIGGLE WORM
continued

4. Drill the off-centered axle holes on the *inside* face of six wheels using the dimensions on the Wheel detail on *page 15.* (See the Buying Guide, *opposite,* for our source of wheels and other needed parts.)

5. Glue an axle peg in the axle hole of all eight wheels. After the glue has dried, saw off the peg shaft protruding from the inside face of each wheel.

6. Drill a ¼"-diameter hole ½" deep centered on the inside face of the two wheels you selected for the head segment.

7. Crosscut four 4" lengths of ¼" dowel for the axles. Sand a slight chamfer on each end. Glue one end of three of the dowels in the offset axle holes drilled in three wheels, and one in the redrilled center of one of the head segment wheels.

Make the antennae and eyes

1. To make the antennae cams (C), crosscut two ¹¹⁄₁₆" lengths from a 1¼"-diameter dowel. If you don't have a dowel this size, you can cut them using a circle cutter or scrollsaw from ¾" scrap. Next, tape the cams together end for end. Using dimensions on the Cam detail, locate the centerpoint for the ¹⁷⁄₆₄" hole. Drill the hole through both pieces. Separate the cams, remove the tape, and then insert a ¼" dowel through the cam holes. Offset the cams 180° as shown on the Head detail. Now, glue the cams together (but not to the dowel) in that offset position. After the glue sets, remove the cam assembly from the dowel.

2. For the two antennae (see the Antenna detail), cross-cut two 2¾" lengths of ⁵⁄₁₆" dowel. Next, place a ¾" wood ball in a hand-screw clamp, and using a ⁵⁄₁₆" bit, drill a ¼"-deep hole. (We sanded one side to flatten it, and drilled into that area.) Drill the second ball.

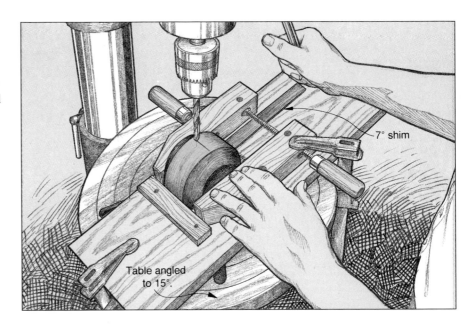

7° shim

Table angled to 15°.

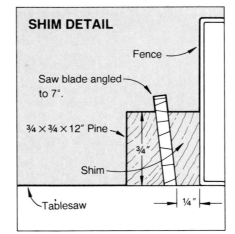

SHIM DETAIL

Fence

Saw blade angled to 7°.

¾ × ¾ × 12" Pine

¾"

Shim

Tablesaw

¼"

CHAMFER DETAIL

Ⓐ

⅞"

⅞"

Ⓑ

Body segment

⅞" piloted chamfer bit

⅞"

Router table

3. Sand to flatten one face on the ½" wood balls, and then drill a ¹⁄₁₆" hole through both. Carefully glue and screw a ball to one end of each antenna dowel as shown in the Antenna detail (we used #3×¾" roundhead wood screws). Do not attach the balls to the other end of the dowels yet.

4. To make the eyes, crosscut the shafts on two ⁷⁄₃₂" toy axle pegs to ⅜" long. Glue a ⅜" axle cap onto the heads of each axle peg. Put them aside for painting.

Time to finish and assemble your worm

1. Finish-sand all parts and then apply the finish of your choice. (We applied two coats of lacquer, sanding after each coat with 320-grit sandpaper.) Finish the eyes. (We stained half of each axle cap, and painted the other half white. After that coat dried, we painted the pupil areas black.)

2. To assemble the head, turn the segment upside down, and insert both antennae through the antennae holes from inside the

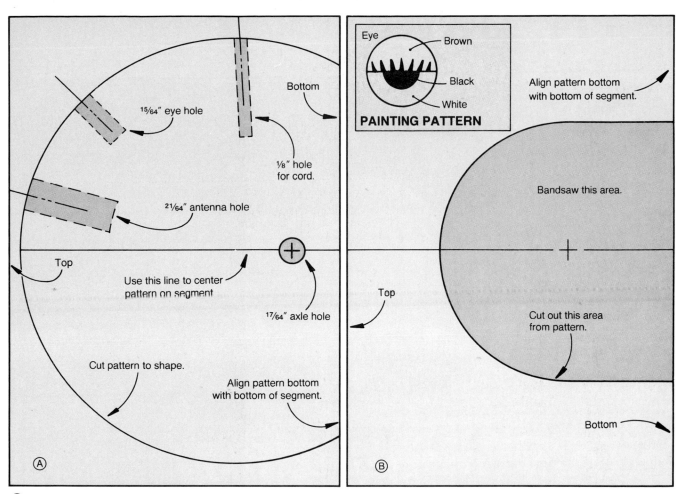

A Template   **FULL-SIZED PATTERNS**   **B** Template

cavity. Pick up the assembled front axle and wheel, slip a ¼" zinc washer over the dowel, and then insert the dowel through the axle hole drilled in the segment's side. Next, place the cams inside the cavity and slide the axle dowel through the cams. Now, pass the end of the dowel through the axle hole in the other side, place a washer over the axle, and glue on the other front wheel.

3. Center the cams on the axle within the cavity. Nail the cams to the axle with #14x½" brads.

4. Turn the head over and glue the drilled ¾" balls on the ends of both antenna dowels. Glue the eyes (axle pegs) in the eye holes.

5. Assemble the wheels and axles on the remaining body segments as shown on the Exploded View drawing. Position the paired wheels so they offset each other 180°.

6. Locate a centerpoint for the screw eyes in the center of the segments and 1" up from the bottom. Drill ¹⁄₁₆" pilot holes, and then screw a ¼" screw eye into each of these holes. Next, line up the segments, and using a needle-nose pliers, bend the loop of one of the paired screw eyes open. Now, hook the opposing screw eyes together, and then close the open loops.

7. Clamp a 1½"-diameter wood ball in a wood screw clamp and drill a ⅛" hole through the center. Next, thread a 15" length of ⅛" nylon cord through the hole in the ball and the head. Now, tie knots on both ends of the cord.

Buying Guide
• **Worm kit.** Includes the required wood wheels, toy axle pegs, axle caps, wood balls, and screw eyes. Kit no. 9200.

For current prices, contact Meisel Hardware Specialties, P.O. Box 70, Mound, MN 55364-0700, or call 800-441-9870.

Project Tool List
Tablesaw
Bandsaw
Disc sander
Router
   Router table
   Chamfer bit
Drill
Drill press
   Bits: ¹⁄₁₆", ⅛", ¼", ⁵⁄₁₆", ¹⁵⁄₆₄", ¹⁷⁄₆₄", ²¹⁄₆₄"
Finishing sander

Note: *We built the project using the tools listed. You may be able to substitute other tools or equipment for listed items you don't have. Additional common tools and clamps may be required to complete the project.*

17

PATTY APATOSAURUS

We fell in love with this pull toy the first time we peeked at entries in *WOOD*® magazine's Build-A-Toy™ contest. Through the magic of canvas sandwiched between pine, our favorite rolling creature will wiggle into your heart, too. (You may recognize this shape as a brontosaurus, but dinosaur experts now prefer Apatosaurus. That's scientific progress!)

Cut the wood parts first

Note: We cut the 36 parts listed on the Bill of Materials from one ¾×9¼×96" piece of clear pine. See the Cutting Diagram opposite for how we laid out the parts.

1. Crosscut the stock at 41" to separate the section for parts A, B, and C from the remaining stock. Set the longer piece aside.

2. Tilt your tablesaw blade 15° from vertical, and rip a 3"-wide piece from the 41"-long stock. (Part A requires a bevel on only one edge.) Now, set this 3"-wide piece aside temporarily; you'll do the crosscutting later.

3. Without changing the blade setting, move the fence 1¾" from the inside of the blade (measured at the table surface). Turn the beveled edge of the remaining 41"-long piece against the fence as shown at *far right* on the Bevel Set-up drawing *opposite*, and bevel-rip one strip. (When crosscut later, this piece will yield four B parts.) Next, position the fence 2" from the blade, and bevel-rip two strips. (You'll cut six C parts from these two strips.)

4. Using the same procedures, bevel-rip the remaining 55"-long piece of stock into 1½"-wide strips for the D parts. (To bevel the first edge, we initially set the fence ¾" from the blade.)

5. Reset your saw blade perpendicular to the saw table. Clamp a clearance block to your rip fence, and set it to crosscut 10" lengths. Next, crosscut the 3"-wide strip into four A parts, and the 1¾"-wide strip into four B parts. Crosscut six C parts from the two 2"-wide strips, and finally, crosscut 22 D parts from the 1½"-wide strips. (We penciled the appropriate letter on each piece as we cut them to aid in laying out the dinosaur later.)

6. Cut two pieces of ¼" plywood to 10×32". Apply double-faced tape to the face of one piece as shown on the Assembly drawing *opposite*. Next, cut a 10×32" piece of lightweight canvas fabric. (We purchased our canvas material at a fabric store.)

7. Starting at the head, place the first layer of parts face down on the board in the order shown by our Assembly and Layout drawings

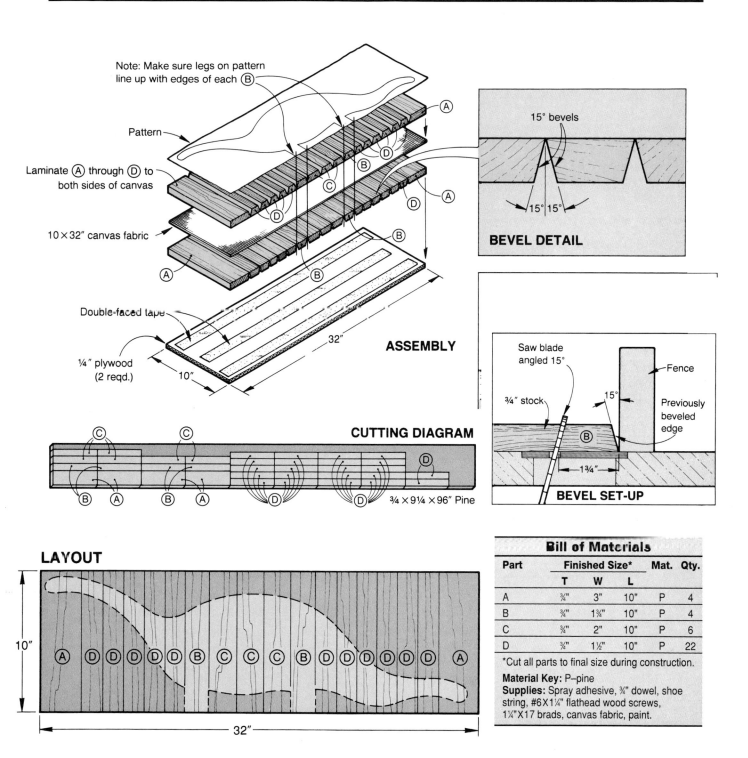

Note: Make sure legs on pattern line up with edges of each Ⓑ

Pattern

Laminate Ⓐ through Ⓓ to both sides of canvas

10×32″ canvas fabric

Double-faced tape

¼″ plywood (2 reqd.)

10″

32″

ASSEMBLY

15° bevels

15° 15°

BEVEL DETAIL

Saw blade angled 15°

¾″ stock

Fence

15°

Previously beveled edge

1¾″

BEVEL SET-UP

CUTTING DIAGRAM

¾ X 9¼ X 96″ Pine

LAYOUT

10″

Ⓐ Ⓓ Ⓓ Ⓓ Ⓓ Ⓓ Ⓑ Ⓒ Ⓒ Ⓒ Ⓑ Ⓓ Ⓓ Ⓓ Ⓓ Ⓓ Ⓓ Ⓐ

32″

Bill of Materials				
Part	Finished Size*		Mat.	Qty.
	T	W	L		
A	¾″	3″	10″	P	4
B	¾″	1¾″	10″	P	4
C	¾″	2″	10″	P	6
D	¾″	1½″	10″	P	22

*Cut all parts to final size during construction.

Material Key: P–pine
Supplies: Spray adhesive, ¾″ dowel, shoe string, #6X1¼″ flathead wood screws, 1¼″X17 brads, canvas fabric, paint.

above. Position the parts firmly against each other, and then square them with the bottom of the plywood carrier board.

8. Apply an even coat of glue to the back sides of the pine pieces. (We rolled on yellow woodworker's glue with a short-nap 3″ paint roller.) Next, lay the canvas fabric on the glued surface, and

then smooth out the material with your hands. Now, apply a coat of glue to the canvas surface using the paint roller as described earlier.

9. Place the remaining wood dinosaur pieces on top of the canvas in order. Make sure each piece matches a comparable piece on the opposite side of the canvas, and that the joints line up. Place the second

plywood piece over the lamination, clamp, and let set overnight.

Cut the pattern and watch a dinosaur take shape

1. While the lamination dries, make a gridded dinosaur pattern. First, tape sheets of paper end to end to form one length measuring
continued

PATTY APATOSAURUS
continued

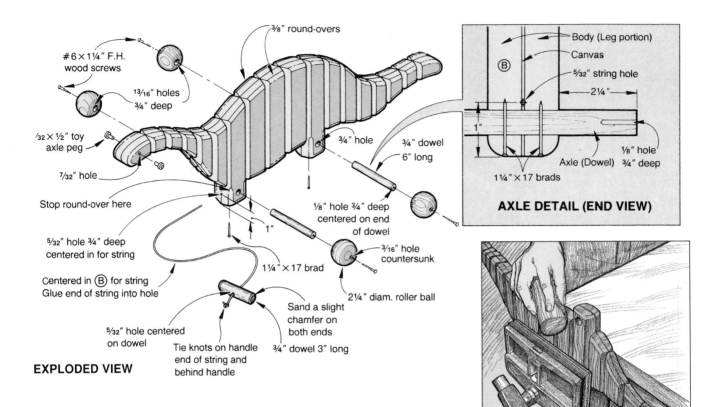

#6 × 1¼" F.H. wood screws

³⁄₈" round-overs

Body (Leg portion)

Canvas

⁵⁄₃₂" string hole

2¼"

¹³⁄₁₆" holes ¾" deep

1"

³⁄₃₂ × ½" toy axle peg

¾" hole

¾" dowel 6" long

Axle (Dowel)

⅛" hole ¾" deep

⁷⁄₃₂" hole

1¼" × 17 brads

AXLE DETAIL (END VIEW)

Stop round-over here

⅛" hole ¾" deep centered on end of dowel

⁵⁄₃₂" hole ¾" deep centered in for string

1"

Centered in Ⓑ for string Glue end of string into hole

1¼" × 17 brad

³⁄₁₆" hole countersunk

2¼" diam. roller ball

⁵⁄₃₂" hole centered on dowel

Sand a slight chamfer on both ends

¾" dowel 3" long

Tie knots on handle end of string and behind handle

EXPLODED VIEW

10" wide by 32" long. Starting at one corner, draw 1" squares across the entire surface.

2. Using the Gridded Dinosaur pattern *opposite* as your guide, draw the dinosaur outline on your gridded sheet. (When working with gridded patterns, we first plot the points where the pattern lines cross the grid lines. Then, we draw the lines to connect the points. We find French curves helpful in drawing smooth, curving lines.) Don't forget to mark the eye and axle-hole centerpoints on your pattern.

3. With scissors, cut out the paper pattern, leaving a ½" margin around the edges.

4. After the glue dries, remove the clamps from the lamination. Apply spray adhesive to the back-side of the pattern, and adhere it to the face of the lamination. (We aligned the pattern and lamination by matching the B parts.) Mark the

eye and axle centerpoints with an awl or nail.

5. With both carrier boards still attached to the lamination, cut the dinosaur body to shape. (We used a portable electric sabersaw and carefully sawed just outside the line.) Now, remove the carrier boards, clamp the dinosaur in your vise, and sand the sawed edges as shown *above right*. (We used 100-grit sandpaper for this.)

6. Mount a ⁷⁄₃₂" bit in your drill press and drill a hole in scrap. Test-fit your toy axle pegs in this hole; we've found that the diameter of these parts vary. See the Buying Guide for our source of wheels and toy axle pegs. When you're satisfied with the fit, drill the eyehole all the way through the head. Next, bore the two ¾" axle holes through the body where marked.

7. Rout a ⅜" round-over along all edges of the dinosaur as shown

opposite. Next, cut two 6"-long axles from a ¾" dowel.

8. Apply a bead of yellow woodworker's glue around the center of each axle, and insert them in the axle holes. Center the axles. Next, snip off the head of a 1¼"×17 brad and with it drill pilot holes where shown in the Axle detail above. Drive a brad in each hole, set them, and fill the holes. (We used Durham's Rock Hard Putty.) When dry, sand the putty smooth.

Apply paint and take your friend on a test drive

1. Prime all surfaces. (We applied a coat of all-purpose primer.) When dry, sand the primer lightly with 220-grit sandpaper. (Before spraying, we fished a coat hanger through the eye holes, then flexed and bent the body and tail as we painted. This enabled us to

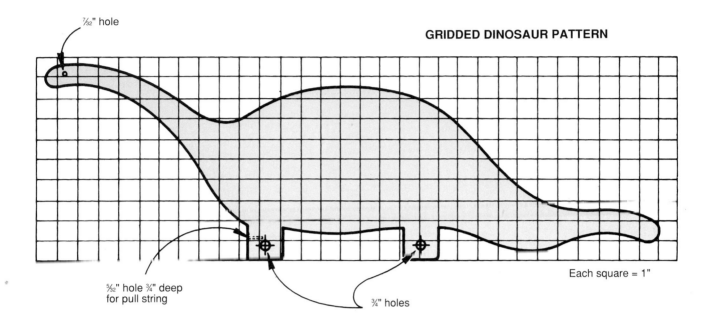

⁷⁄₃₂" hole

GRIDDED DINOSAUR PATTERN

⁵⁄₃₂" hole ¾" deep
for pull string

¾" holes

Each square = 1"

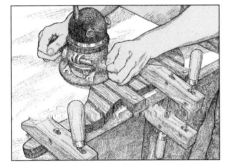

get paint onto all sides and surfaces of the body segments.) Next, apply the top coat. (We spray-applied a lime-green enamel paint.)

2. Shorten the shafts on two toy axle pegs to ½". Paint the peg heads white. After they dry, paint the center circle of the pegs black to represent the pupil. Now, glue and insert the axle-peg eyes in the holes drilled into the head.

3. To prepare the wheels, clamp one of the 2¼"-diameter roller balls in a handscrew clamp with the predrilled hole facing up. (We found the toy was less likely to tip with these wider wheels. Also, we taped strips of sandpaper to the inside faces of the clamp to hold

the balls.) Next, center the hole in the ball under a ¹³⁄₁₆" spade bit in your drill press, and enlarge the hole to a depth of ¾". (We ground about ¹⁄₁₆" off the tip on each corner on the bit to round the bottom of the hole.) Bore the axle holes in the other three roller balls the same way. Switch to a ³⁄₁₆" bit, center it in the hole, and drill the rest of the way through each ball. Finally, turn over each ball, and countersink the screw holes in the outside face.

4. Slide the wheels onto the axles, insert a ⅛" drill bit through the holes in the wheels, and drill ¾" into the axle ends. Rub paraffin wax onto the ends of the axles, place the wheels over the axles again, and drive a #6x1¼" screw through each wheel and into the axle. Tighten all screws just enough to keep the wheels from wobbling.

5. Crosscut a 3" length of ¾" dowel, chamfer the ends, and drill a ⁵⁄₃₂" hole through the center. Drill the same-size hole in the center of the front leg (B) where shown on the Exploded View. Apply finish to the dowel. Next, knot one end of your pull string (we used a 24"

leather-like shoe lace), thread it through the dowel hole, and tie another knot. Now, glue (we used cyanoacrylate glue) the free end of the string in the hole you just drilled into the shoulder.

Buying Guide

• **Dinosaur kit.** Four 2¼" roller balls, and two ⁷⁄₃₂" toy axle pegs. Kit no. 9835. For current prices, contact Meisel Hardware Specialties, P.O. Box 70, Mound, MN 55364-0700, or call 800-441-9870.

Project Tool List
Tablesaw
Sabersaw
Router
    ⅜" round-over bit
Drill
Drill Press
    Bits: ⅛", ⁵⁄₃₂", ⁷⁄₃₂", ¾", ¹³⁄₁₆"
Finishing sander

Note: *We built the project using the tools listed. You may be able to substitute other tools or equipment for listed items you don't have. Additional common tools and clamps may be required to complete the project.*

UDDERLY FUNNY ROCKING COW

The instant you set this bovine beauty rocking, you'll find yourself laughing till the cows come home. Once in motion, our holstein's tail, udder, and head wag pendulum-like from side to side, but not together. Use our patterns and scrollsaw or bandsaw the parts.

We'll cut out the parts first

1. Using carbon paper or a photo-copier, make copies of the full-sized patterns on *pages 24* and *25*. Include the centerpoints for all holes. Now, cut the patterns to rough shape with scissors, leaving about a ¼" margin around the edges.

2. Select your wood stock. (We chose ¾"-thick clear pine [except for the base] to avoid having to work around knots.)

3. Again using carbon paper, transfer the cow patterns you made in Step 1 onto the face of the stock as shown *below*. Mark the center-points for all drill holes on each piece with an awl. (See the Cutting Diagram on *page 25* for sugges-tions on how we laid out the

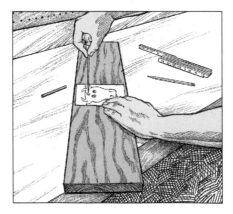

patterns for grain direction.) If you made photocopies of the patterns, cut them out with scissors, spray the backs with spray adhesive, and adhere them to the face of the piece.

4. Drill the ⁵⁄₃₂" holes through the cow's head (E) and tail (F) where marked. (We backed all pieces with scrap when drilling holes to prevent chip-out.) Switch bits and drill the ³⁄₃₂" hole through the udder (D) piece. Next, drill the ⁷⁄₃₂" holes through the back legs (A) and the front legs (C) pieces where marked. Change bits again and drill the ⅛" hole ½" deep on the inside face of the back legs.

5. Cut the individual cow parts (A, B, C, D, E, F) to shape. (To simplify the task, we first rough-cut each part from the others, and then sawed them to shape.)

6. Crosscut the stock for the rockers into two 12" lengths. Using double-faced tape, stick the pieces together face to face. Trace the rocker pattern (G) onto the face of one piece. With your drill press, drill the two ¼" holes through both pieces.

7. Saw the rockers to shape. (We used a bandsaw equipped with a ⅛" blade to cut out the parts but a scrollsaw will work. We cut outside of the line.)

8. Rip and crosscut the 5×5" base (H) piece. (We cut ours from ¼"-thick mahogany but any thin plywood will work.)

9. Crosscut two ¼"-diameter dowels to 5¼" long. Cut one 1¹¹⁄₁₆" length of ⅛" dowel. Set them aside.

Next, sand and rout the parts

1. Sand the cut edges on all parts. (We used a 1" belt sander as shown *opposite* to sand the cow's body parts, and a drum sander to sand the rockers.) Sand one face of the udder to remove about ¹⁄₁₆" of thickness.

(We thinned ours on a belt sander.) Now, separate the rocker pieces and remove the tape.

2. Chuck a ¼" round-over bit in your table-mounted router. Round over the edges on the cow parts. (For safety, we suggest you round over the tail, and around the horns and ears on the head by hand. We used a ⅛" rasp and a ³⁄₁₆" half-round mill bastard file to smooth and round over the cuts in these areas, and a drum sander to help shape the tail.) Always use a protective guard, and hold the pieces so your fingers remain a safe distance from the rotating bit.

3. Round over the edges on the rockers with the same bit. Using a countersink bit, slightly enlarge the ¼" holes on the faces of both rocker pieces. Next, sand all parts with 150-grit sandpaper.

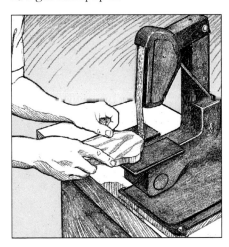

Paint and assemble your rocking cow

1. Paint the cow parts (including two toy axle pegs), the rocker, and the base. Because no two cows ever have identical black and white patterns, feel free to develop your own painting pattern. (We used acrylic paint, making the base and rocker an antique red color, and the cow black and white. After painting, let the parts dry well before assembling the cow.

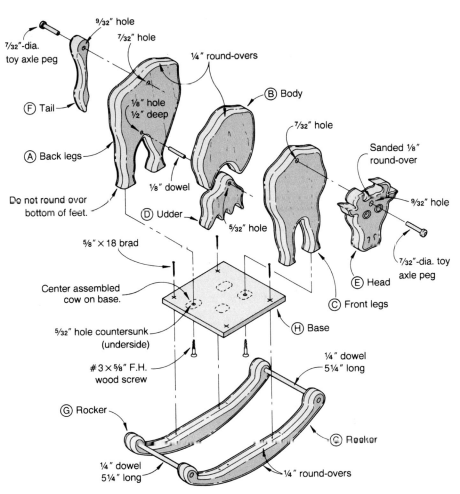

⁹⁄₃₂" hole

⁷⁄₃₂" hole

⁷⁄₃₂"-dia. toy axle peg

¼" round-overs

Ⓕ Tail

Ⓑ Body

⅛" hole ½" deep

⁷⁄₃₂" hole

Ⓐ Back legs

Sanded ⅛" round-over

⅛" dowel

⁹⁄₃₂" hole

Do not round over bottom of feet.

Ⓓ Udder

⁵⁄₃₂" hole

⁷⁄₃₂"-dia. toy axle peg

⅝" × 18 brad

Ⓔ Head

Ⓒ Front legs

Center assembled cow on base.

Ⓗ Base

⁵⁄₃₂" hole countersunk (underside)

¼" dowel 5¼" long

#3 × ⅝" F.H. wood screw

Ⓖ Rocker

Ⓖ Rocker

¼" dowel 5¼" long

¼" round-overs

2. Glue and assemble the rockers. (We used yellow woodworker's glue.) Place the base on the rockers, and nail with four #18X⅝" brads.

3. To assemble the cow, first lay the back legs (A) on a flat surface with the outside face down. (See the Exploded View drawing *above* for reference.) Apply glue to the back side of the body (B) piece. Place it on the top face of the back legs, aligning it along the top and locating it slightly off center as indicated by the broken line on the pattern of A. Next, glue the ⅛" dowel in the hole on the inside face of the back. Place the udder over the ⅛" dowel *but do not glue it*—you want the udder to swing freely.

continued

Bill of Materials

Part	Initial Size*			Mat.	Qty.
	T	**W**	**L**		
A back legs	¾"	5½"	7¾"	P	1
B body	¾"	5"	5"	P	1
C front legs	¾"	4½"	7¾"	P	1
D udder	¾"	3"	3"	P	1
E head	¾"	4½"	4½"	P	1
F tail	¾"	1"	5¼"	P	1
G rocker	¾"	3"	12"	P	2
H base	¼"	5"	5"	MP	1

*Cut parts to finished size during construction. Please read all of the instructions before cutting the material.

Material Key: P—pine, MP—mahogany plywood.

Supplies: ⅛" dowel, ¼" dowel, 2—1¹⁄₁₆" long X⁷⁄₃₂" diameter birch toy axle pegs, acrylic or enamel paints, 2—#3x⅝" flathead wood screws, #18X⅝" wire brads.

UDDERLY FUNNY ROCKING COW
continued

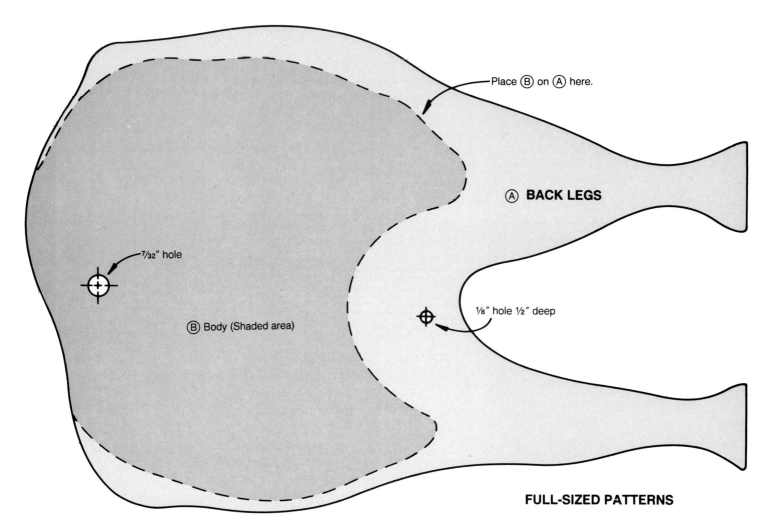

Place Ⓑ on Ⓐ here.

Ⓐ **BACK LEGS**

⁷⁄₃₂" hole

Ⓑ Body (Shaded area)

⅛" hole ½" deep

FULL-SIZED PATTERNS

4. Apply glue to the front face of the body part. Place the front legs (C) on top of part B, and align it, referring to the location suggested on the pattern. Stand the assembly up, and adjust the alignment of the two leg parts so all four feet stand level on a flat surface. Clamp the assembly until the glue sets. (We used spring-type clamps.)

5. Set the cow on the base, position it where you desire, and then lightly trace around one front foot and the opposite back foot with a pencil. Remove the cow, mark centerpoints for the two foot prints you just traced, and then drill and countersink the two ⁵⁄₃₂" holes on the underside.

Place the cow back on the base, align the feet with the outlines, turn the two parts over together, and then mark the screw holes on the feet. With a portable hand drill, drill a ¹⁄₁₆" pilot hole in each foot where marked. Screw the cow to the rocker base.

6. Insert a toy axle peg through the hole in the head, and glue the tip of the peg in the hole in the front legs piece. Allow enough clearance between the head and the front legs piece so the head can swing freely. Attach the tail to the back legs piece the same way. Now, rock the cow and enjoy the action.

Project Tool List
Tablesaw
Bandsaw or scrollsaw
Belt sander
Router
   Router table
   ¼" round-over bit
Drill
   Sanding drum
   Bits: ¹⁄₁₆", ⅛", ⁵⁄₃₂", ⁷⁄₃₂", ¼", ⁹⁄₃₂"
Finishing sander

Note: *We built the project using the tools listed. You may be able to substitute other tools or equipment for listed items you don't have. Additional common tools and clamps may be required to complete the project.*

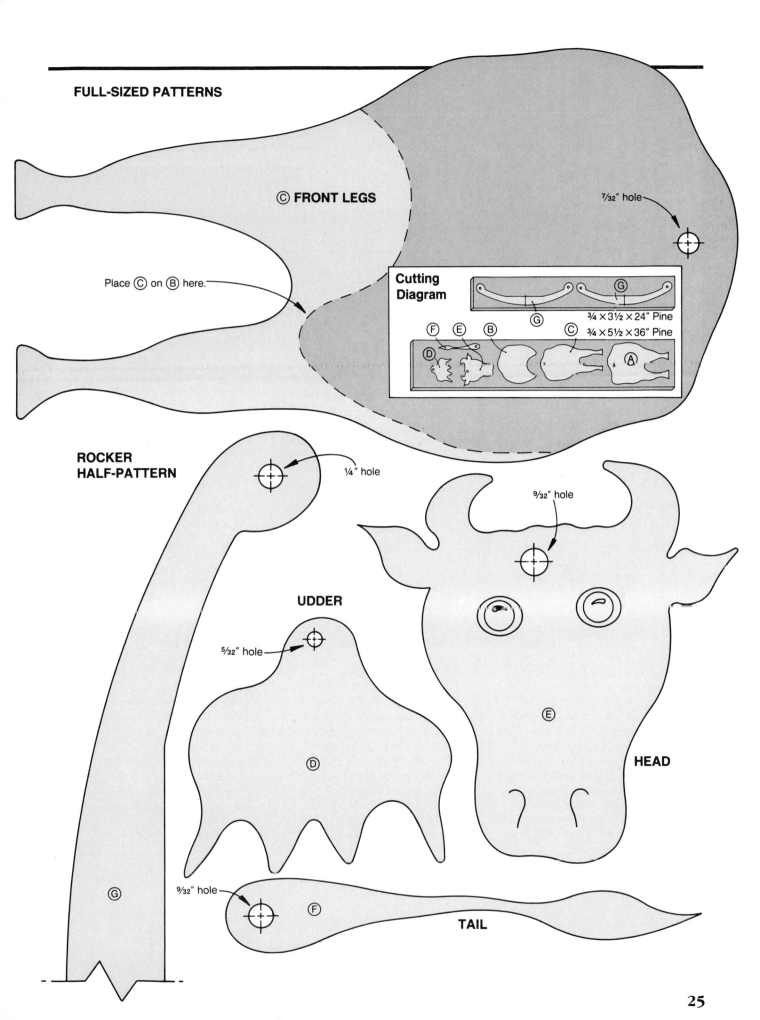

FULL-SIZED PATTERNS

Ⓒ **FRONT LEGS**

⁷⁄₃₂″ hole

Place Ⓒ on Ⓑ here.

Cutting Diagram

Ⓖ

Ⓖ   ¾ × 3½ × 24″ Pine

Ⓕ Ⓔ   Ⓑ   Ⓒ   ¾ × 5½ × 36″ Pine

Ⓓ   Ⓐ

ROCKER HALF-PATTERN

¼″ hole

⁹⁄₃₂″ hole

UDDER

⁵⁄₃₂″ hole

Ⓓ

Ⓔ

HEAD

Ⓖ

⁹⁄₃₂″ hole   Ⓕ

TAIL

25

GIDDYAP ROCKING HORSE

Clippity-clop, clippity-clop—
that's the sound our
galloping horse makes every
time you set it a-rocking. Place
the maned toy rocker shown
above on your child's dresser,
or build our classy rustic
version *above right* and give it
to a country-loving friend.
Either way, you'll ride high in
the saddle with the joy you
bring. Our instructions tell how
to build both.

Note: *This project requires
⅜"-, ½"-, and ¾"-thick stock. You can
resaw or plane thicker stock to the
correct thickness.*

Make the rockers first

1. To make a full-sized rocker
pattern, trace the half-pattern on
page 28 onto a sheet of tracing
paper. Using carbon paper, transfer
the half pattern onto a sheet of
paper; then, flip the pattern, align
the center hole marks, and trace
the other half of the pattern to
complete the rocker. Mark the
centerpoints for all holes and the
dash line for the spacer block. Cut
out the pattern leaving about a
½" paper margin outside the line.

2. To form the rockers (A), rip
and crosscut two pieces of ½"-thick
wood to 4×12". (We used maple
but found it difficult to sand and
stain uniformly.) Stick the two

pieces together with double-faced
tape. Now, spray adhesive to the
back side of your paper rocker
pattern and adhere it to the top
piece. With an awl, mark the
center points for the four holes
to be drilled.

3. Using a bandsaw, cut the
rocker to shape. (We cut just
outside the line and sanded to the
line.) Remove the paper pattern
and sand the bottom of the
rockers on a disk sander (as
shown *below*) by slowly rotating
the pieces. Sand carefully to
maintain a smooth arc on the
rockers. Mount a 1"-diameter drum
sander on the drill press and sand
along the top edges of the rockers.
Hand-sand the sides and places a
drum sander can't reach.

4. Chuck a ⅜" bit in your drill
press and drill the two end holes.
Back the bottom piece with scrap
to prevent chip-out. Separate the
two rockers and remove the tape.

5. To make the rocker spacer (B), rip a ¾"-thick piece of maple to 1-1/16" wide; then, crosscut it to 3⅛" long. Draw diagonals across one end, mark the centerpoint, and drill a ⅜" hole, ¾" deep.

6. From ⅜" dowel stock, cut four 1¾"-long pieces and set two aside for use later. Lay one rocker on its side and apply glue to the inside surface of the two holes. Apply glue to one end of each dowel and insert them into the two holes, flush with the back side. Place a ¾" round wooden bead (the type used for macrame and available at crafts supply stores) over the dowels.

7. Apply glue to one face of the spacer block (B) and position it on the rocker where indicated by the dash line. Make certain the end with the hole is at the top of the rocker. Now, apply glue to the other face of the spacer block, the free ends of the dowels, and to the inside surface of the two end holes in the other rocker. Place the second rocker over the dowels and press it down until it's snug against the spacer block and beads. Test the alignment by rocking it a few times. Adjust and clamp the assembly.

8. Remove the clamps after the glue dries. Then, drill the two previously marked ⅜" holes through the rockers and spacer block. Slightly bevel one end of each of the two remaining ⅜" dowels. Apply glue to the dowels and holes, and tap the dowels through the rockers and the spacer block. Now, sand all dowel ends flush.

Let's make the horse

1. Using carbon paper, transfer the full-sized Horse pattern to a ¾x5x8" piece of maple. (Again, we first transferred the pattern to paper, applied spray adhesive, and stuck the pattern onto the maple piece.) Mark the centerpoints for all drilling locations. If you intend to finish your horse with the yarn mane, mark the location for those holes at this time too.

Note: *Eliminate the horse's ears if you intend to put a mane on it.*

2. Using a bandsaw or scrollsaw, cut the horse body (C) to shape. (Again, we cut just outside the marked line, and later finish-sanded to the line.)

3. Transfer the three full-sized patterns for the legs (D, E, and F) to ⅜"-thick maple. (You may have to sand or plane thicker stock to this thickness.) Now cut the legs to shape. (To save time on the rear

continued

EXPLODED VIEW

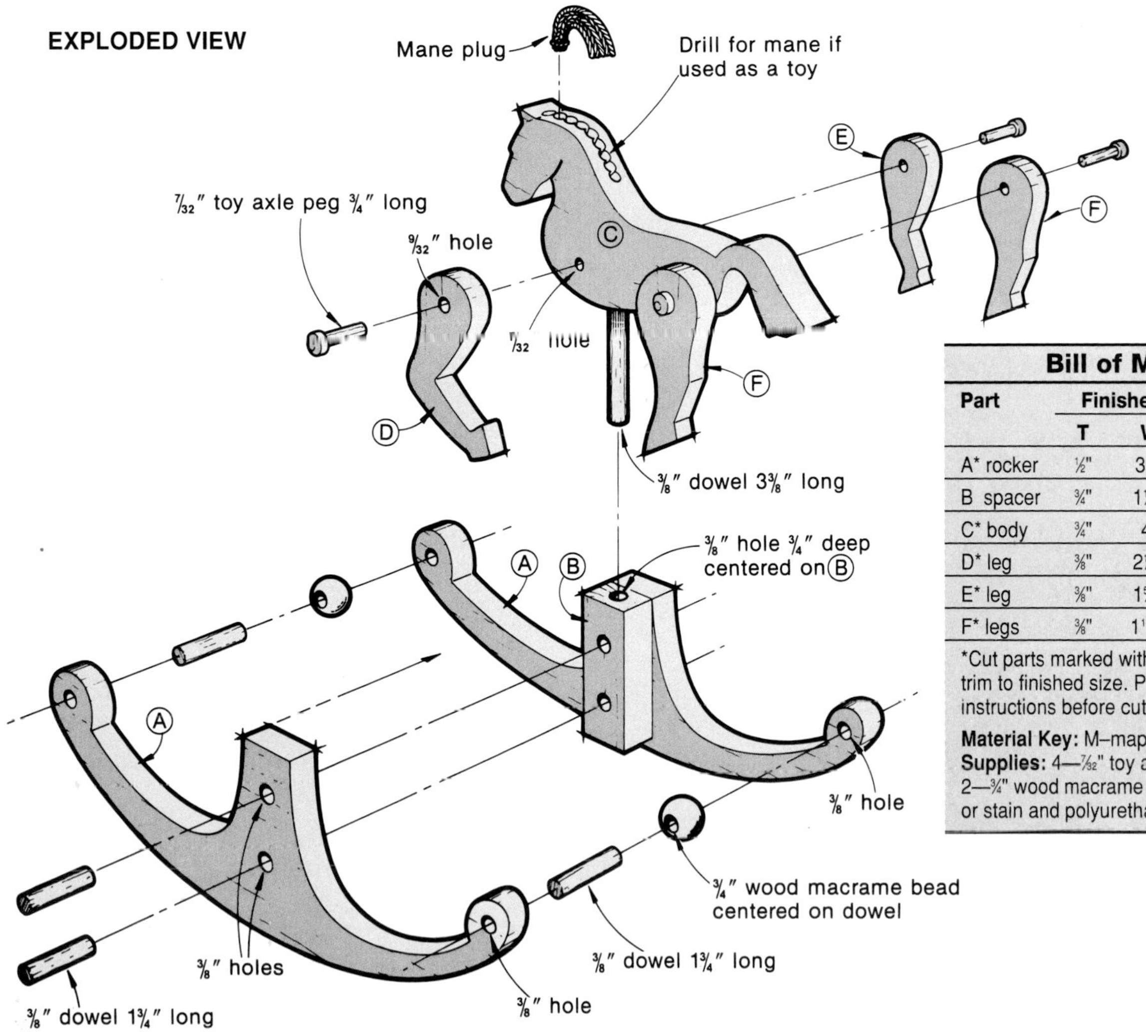

Mane plug
Drill for mane if used as a toy
E
F
C
7/32" toy axle peg ¾" long
9/32" hole
7/32" hole
D
F
⅜" dowel 3⅜" long
⅜" hole ¾" deep centered on B
A
B
A
⅜" hole
¾" wood macrame bead centered on dowel
⅜" holes
⅜" dowel 1¾" long
⅜" hole
⅜" dowel 1¾" long

Bill of Materials

Part	Finished Size*			Mat.	Qty.
	T	W	L		
A* rocker	½"	3¼"	11⅜	M	2
B spacer	¾"	1-1/16"	3⅛"	M	1
C* body	¾"	4"	7⅝"	M	1
D* leg	⅜"	2-1/16"	4"	M	1
E* leg	⅜"	1-5/16"	4-3/16"	M	1
F* legs	⅜"	1-11/16"	4¼"	M	2

*Cut parts marked with an * larger initially and trim to finished size. Please read the instructions before cutting.

Material Key: M–maple

Supplies: 4—7/32" toy axle pegs, ⅜" dowel, 2—¾" wood macrame beads, wool yarn, paint or stain and polyurethane.

GIDDYAP ROCKING HORSE
continued

FULL-SIZED PATTERNS

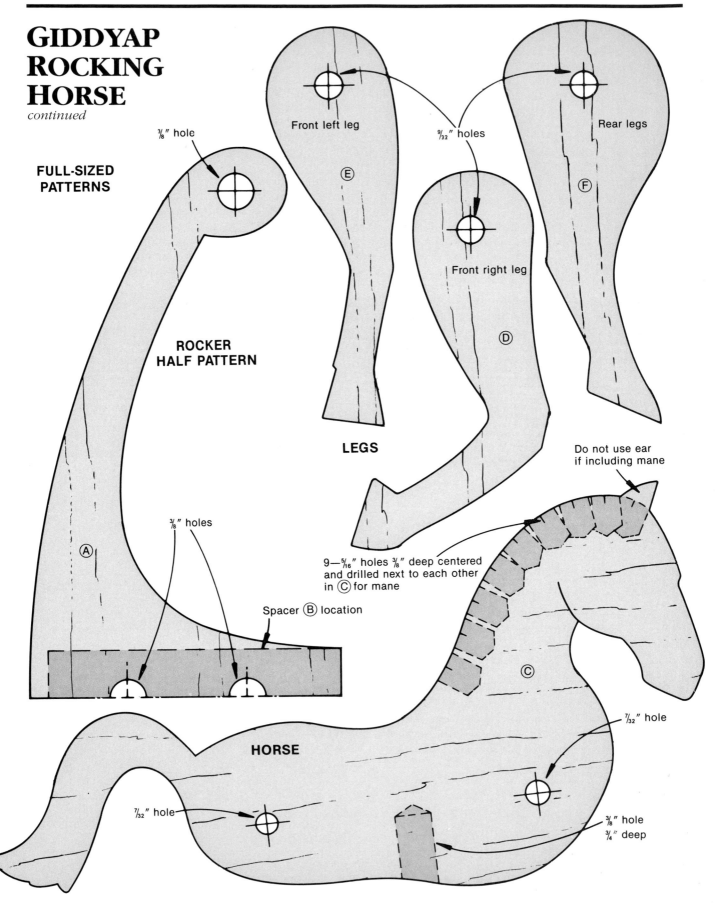

³⁄₈″ hole

Front left leg

⁹⁄₃₂″ holes

Rear legs

Ⓔ

Ⓕ

Front right leg

Ⓓ

ROCKER HALF PATTERN

LEGS

Do not use ear if including mane

9—⁵⁄₁₆″ holes ³⁄₈″ deep centered and drilled next to each other in Ⓒ for mane

Ⓐ

³⁄₈″ holes

Spacer Ⓑ location

Ⓒ

⁷⁄₃₂″ hole

HORSE

⁷⁄₃₂″ hole

³⁄₈″ hole ³⁄₄″ deep

legs, we stacked two pieces of maple together using double-faced tape, glued the pattern to the top, and cut both out at the same time.)

4. Place the horse's body in a woodscrew clamp as shown *below,* and drill the ⅜" hole in the underside for the support dowel. (We first aligned the centerpoint of the hole with the drill bit, tightened the clamp, and clamped the entire setup to the drill press table to keep it from moving. We then bored the hole.) Remove the body from the clamp, change bits, and drill the two ⁷⁄₃₂" holes in the body for the toy axle pegs, backing the piece with scrap to prevent chipout. Change bits again and drill the ⁹⁄₃₂" holes in the leg pieces, backing each piece.

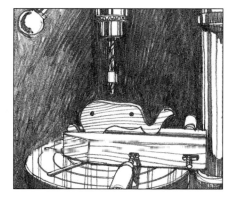

5. Sand the body and leg parts smooth. (We used a ½" drum sander on a drill press to sand the cut surfaces.) Then, sand a slight round-over on all sharp edges.

6. To drill the holes for the mane, chuck a ⁵⁄₆₄" bit in a drill press. Place the horse body in a handscrew clamp as shown *above right,* adjust the body to align each hole with the drill bit, and drill each ⅜" deep.

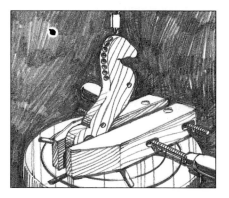

Finishing the Horse

1. Cut a ⅜" dowel 3⅛" long. Apply glue to the hole in the underside of the horse body and insert the dowel. Apply glue to the hole in the spacer block on the rocker and insert the other end of the dowel in it.

2. Finish-sand the horse and rockers. (Apply the finish of your choice. For the toy version, we applied a medium brown stain to all parts except the spacer beads— they were stained with a dark walnut for contrast. Then we applied two coats of polyurethane. The dowels and axle pegs appear darker in color because of the end grain.) See Step 5 for directions on completing the country version.

3. Cut the shafts of four ⁷⁄₃₂ x1⅛" toy axle pegs (sometimes sold as ⅛" pegs) to ¾" long. Use them to mount the legs to the body after you've finished it. Insert the axle pegs through the leg holes, apply glue to the ends of the pegs, and insert the ends into the holes in the horse's body. Allow some play so the legs swing easily.

4. To make the mane for the toy version, wrap wool yarn around a 3x5" card 12 times. Slide the yarn

off the card and tie it in a bundle near the middle with a short piece of yarn. Then, tie another short length of yarn around the bundle about ¼" away from the first tie. With scissors, cut the yarn between the two ties to make two plugs. (You'll need a plug for each hole.) Now, cut through the loops so you have 24 pieces of yarn tied on one end. Apply a small amount of glue into each ⁵⁄₆₄" hole. Using a ¼" dowel, push the knotted end of a yarn into each hole. After the glue dries, clip the mane to the desired shape.

5. To create the country version of the horse, paint all parts. (We applied two coats of rusty-red flat latex.) After the paint dries, sand the horse lightly to remove some of the paint and give it a worn or used look. (After sanding, the exposed wood on our horse looked too light, so we rubbed a light brown stain over those areas. This gave the wood a desirable aged look.)

Project Tool List
Tablesaw
Bandsaw or scrollsaw
Disc sander
Drill Press
    Sanding drum
    Bits: ⁷⁄₃₂", ⁹⁄₃₂", ⁵⁄₆₄", ⅜"
Finishing sander

Note: *We built the project using the tools listed. You may be able to substitute other tools or equipment for listed items you don't have. Additional common tools and clamps may be required to complete the project.*

ONE HONEY OF A BEE

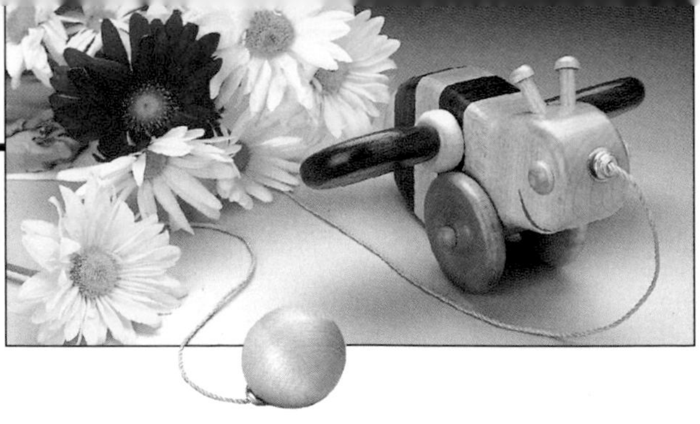

You'll make a beeline to your workshop once you see how easy this pull toy goes together. Maple and walnut laminations create the striped honeybee look in the body, while two sets of wheels give a lively spin to the walnut wings. Pop-off snaps on both ends of the pull cord ensure safety, making this project ideal for young children.

Make the body block first

1. Rip a 12" length of 3/4"-thick walnut to 1 5/16" width, then crosscut two pieces 3 5/8" long. Rip a 24" length of 3/4"-thick maple to the same width. Cross-cut six pieces 3 5/8" long.

2. Laminate the walnut and maple pieces together face to face by first laying them on their edges in the order shown on the Exploded View drawing *below*. Apply wood glue evenly to all mating faces, then carefully align all edges and clamp the assembly. When dry, remove the clamp, and sand the sides of the lamination to 1 1/4"-finished thickness.

3. Using carbon paper, transfer the full-size Bee pattern *opposite* onto the lamination, and mark the hole centerpoints. Carefully cut the bee's body (A) to shape with either a bandsaw or scrollsaw.

4. To make the wings (B), plane or resaw a 3/4x2 1/2x12" piece of walnut to 1/2" thickness. Transfer the full-size (half) Wing pattern and all lines onto the walnut, then flip pattern to double it. Cut the wing part to shape. Do not cut the wings apart yet—it will be safer handling them as one piece when routing the edges. Drum-sand the edges on the wing part and body.

Now, machine the parts

1. Rout a 1/4" round-over along the top and bottom edges of the wing part as shown *below*. Now, saw along the indicated cutoff lines to separate the two wings.

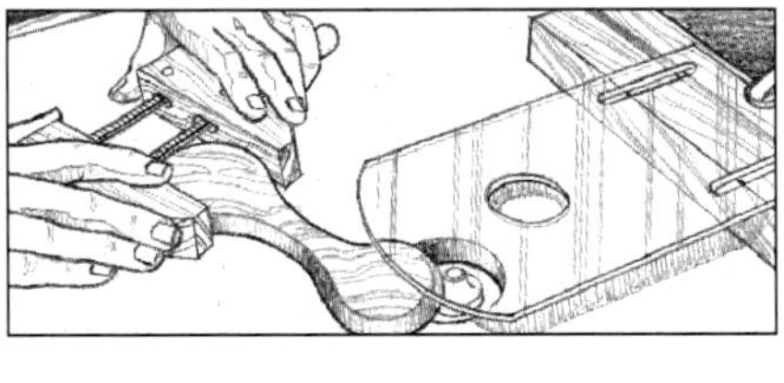

2. Stand the two wing pieces on end and clamp them together. Turn this assembly over, then mark the centers of both wings on the cut ends. Drill a 1/4" dowel hole 1/2" deep in each wing where shown on the Wing pattern.

3. Using a 3/4" Forstner or spade bit, bore the hole for the wing dowel through the body. (We backed the bee's body with scrap to prevent chipout.) Switch bits and drill the 3/8" hole through the body for the eyes. Switch to a 5/16" bit and drill the axle hole.

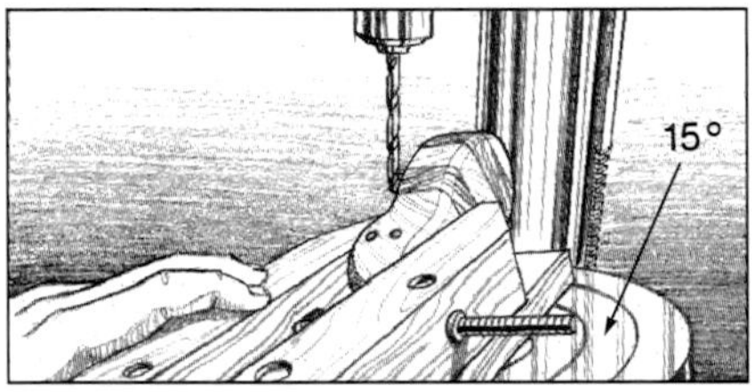
15°

4. To drill the holes for the antennae, clamp the bee, nose down, as shown *above*. Measure in 5/16" from the sides on the top edge where indicated on the full-size Bee pattern, and mark the centerpoints for the antennae. Tilt the drill press table to 15° *left* of center, and with the head facing you, drill the *right* (your right) antennae hole. Tilt the drill press table 15° *right* of center and drill the *left* antennae hole. Level the drill press table, clamp the body, tail up, and drill the hole for the stinger (here, a wood axle peg).

5. Drill a 3/32" pilot hole in a 1 1/2"-diameter wood ball and the bee's nose for the snap fastener screws. (See the Buying Guide *opposite* for sources of special parts.)

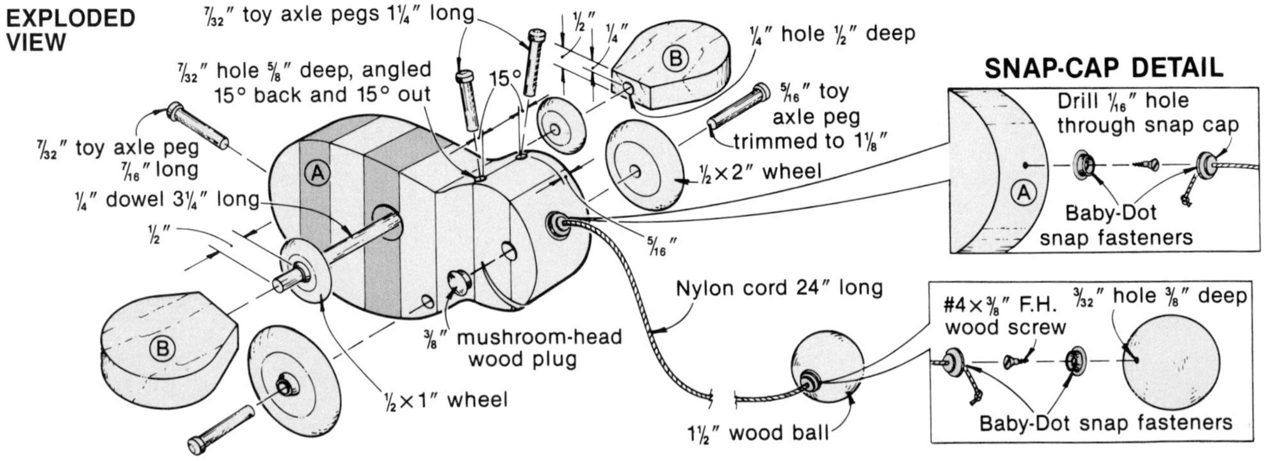
EXPLODED VIEW
7/32" toy axle pegs 1 1/4" long
1/2"
1/4"
7/32" hole 5/8" deep, angled 15° back and 15° out
15°
B
1/4" hole 1/2" deep
5/16" toy axle peg trimmed to 1 1/8"
7/32" toy axle peg 7/16" long
A
1/2x2" wheel
1/4" dowel 3 1/4" long
1/2"
5/16"
Nylon cord 24" long
3/8" mushroom-head wood plug
1/2x1" wheel
1 1/2" wood ball
SNAP-CAP DETAIL
Drill 1/16" hole through snap cap
Baby-Dot snap fasteners
#4x3/8" F.H. wood screw
3/32" hole 3/8" deep
Baby-Dot snap fasteners

Assembling and finishing

1. Finish-sand all of the parts.

2. Glue a ⅜" wood mushroom head plug (also called a wood button) in the eye holes. Glue and tap the ⁷⁄₃₂" axle pegs in place for the antenna, letting them extend ⅝" above the head. Cut the shaft of a ⁷⁄₃₂" axle peg to ⁷⁄₁₆" length and glue the peg in the stinger hole.

3. Apply a nontoxic finish to all parts. (We applied two coats of polyurethane.)

4. Cut a length of ¼" dowel to 3¼". Insert it through the ¾" body hole, center it side to side, and glue a 1" wheel on each side where shown on the Exploded View drawing. Allow ¹⁄₁₆" clearance between each wheel and the bee's body so the wheels can turn easily. Glue and align a wing on each end of the dowel.

5. Cut off the shafts of two ⁵⁄₁₆" toy axle pegs to 1⅛". Insert the pegs through the holes of the 2" wheels, and glue them in the axle holes. Allow ¹⁄₁₆" clearance so the wheels turn freely.

6. Install the Baby-Dot snap fasteners for the pull cord where shown in the Snap-Cap detail on the Exploded View drawing. First, screw the male snap components to the wood ball and bee's nose, driving the screws into the pilot holes drilled earlier. Next, drill ¹⁄₁₆" holes through the female caps. Thread the cord (we used mason line) through these holes and knot the tips. (For clearance in the snaps, we made tiny knots and trimmed the excess cord.)

Buying Guide

• **Wood parts kit.** The wooden wheels, axle pegs, wood plugs, and ball required for the bee can be purchased as a complete kit. For current price of Honeybee Pull Toy Kit, contact Meisel Hardware Specialties, P.O. Box 70, Mound, MN 55364-0700, or call 800-441-9870.

• **Baby-Dot snap fasteners.** Catalog no. 1262, gold tone, pkg. of 10. Tandy Leather. For location of nearest store or for catalog, call 800-433-5546.

Supplies

2— #4x⅜" flathead wood screws, ¼" dowel, 2" cord.

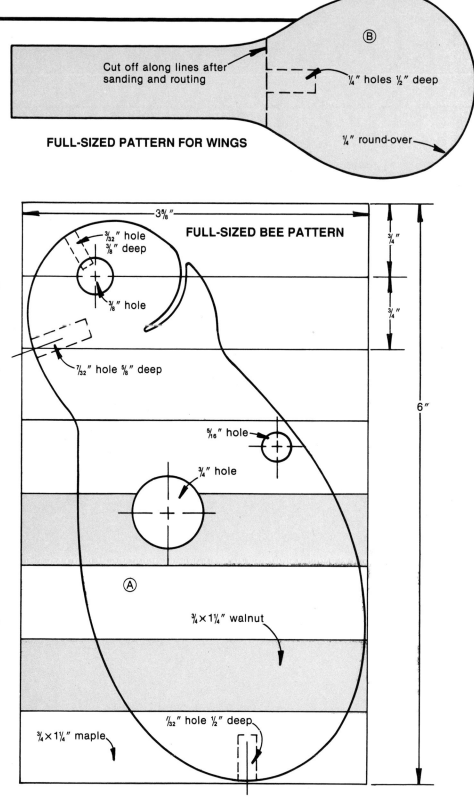

FULL-SIZED PATTERN FOR WINGS

Cut off along lines after sanding and routing

¼" holes ½" deep

ⓑ

¼" round-over

FULL-SIZED BEE PATTERN

¾"

¾"

6"

3⅝"

³⁄₃₂" hole ⅜" deep

⅜" hole

⁷⁄₃₂" hole ⅝" deep

⁵⁄₁₆" hole

¾" hole

ⓐ

¾ × 1¼" walnut

¾ × 1¼" maple

⁷⁄₃₂" hole ½" deep

Project Tool List

Tablesaw
Bandsaw or scrollsaw
Router
    ¼" round-over bit
Drill press
    Bits: ¹⁄₁₆", ³⁄₃₂", ⁷⁄₃₂", ¼", ⁵⁄₁₆", ⅜", ¾"
Finishing sander

Note: We built the project using the tools listed. You may be able to substitute other tools or equipment for listed items you don't have. Additional common tools and clamps may be required to complete the project.

TRAINS AND BOATS AND PLANES, ETC.

Here's a group of toys with plenty of get-up-and-go. Whether chugging down the train track, racing to the finish line, or sailing a soapy sea, this rugged crew will work hard all through your child's playtime.

THE HEAVY HAULIN' LOADER

Our latest piece of heavy equipment may be pint-sized, but this tough-as-nails toy will be big with the sandbox set. Its pivoting-bucket assembly, in the skillful hands of an imaginative child, will move "mountains" of material.

Note: You'll need thin stock for this project. You can either plane or resaw thicker stock to size.

First, the cab and chassis

1. Cut a piece of ¾" pine to 2⅛" wide by 12" long for the cab (A).

2. Measuring 1" from each end of the pine, mark the locations for a pair of 1⅜"-wide dadoes. Using your tablesaw and a miter gauge, cut the dadoes ½" deep where shown in the drawing *above right*.

3. Crosscut the pine into two equal lengths. Mark the windshield location on one piece (see the Window detail on *page 34* for reference). Mark the top of the windshield flush with the top of the dado. Now, drill four ¼" holes at each corner on the inside of the marked windshield. Cut the opening to shape with a scrollsaw or coping saw. Sand or file the cut edges of the windshield.

4. Apply glue to the mating surfaces, align the dadoes, and clamp the cab parts. Remove excess glue (we used a chisel) from the cab interior before it dries.

5. Trim the top and bottom of the cab lamination to length where dimensioned on the Window detail on *page 34*. Sand ¼" round-overs along the cab top where shown on the drawing.

6. Cut the chassis (B) to size.

Add the hood and bucket support

1. Glue and clamp two pieces of ¾"-thick pine for the hood (C). Sand ¼" round-overs on the top edges where shown on the Exploded View drawing on *page 34*.

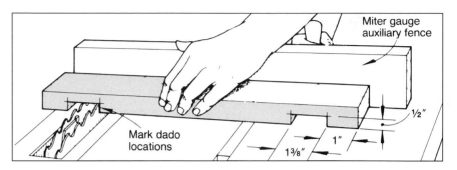

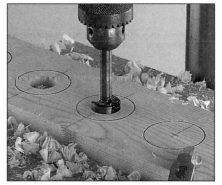

Mark the wheel centerpoint locations 3" apart on the pine, and drill holes ½" deep for each wheel.

Center the circle-cutter pilot bit over the Forstner-bit depression, and cut the wheels to shape.

2. Mark the smokestack and radiator-cap centerpoints, and drill the holes to the sizes stated on the Exploded View drawing.

3. Cut the bucket support (D) to size from 1"-thick pine stock (we laminated two pieces of ½" stock). Mark a ½" radius on one end, and bandsaw it to shape. Mark the centerpoint, and drill

a ¹³⁄₃₂" hole through the support for the bucket pin.

4. Sand the chassis, hood, and support. Spread glue on the mating surfaces, and clamp the support to the front of the chassis, positioning it flush with one end of the chassis and centered from side to side. Next, glue and clamp the *continued*

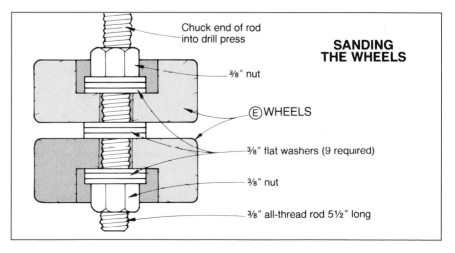

Chuck end of rod into drill press

⅜" nut

Ⓔ WHEELS

⅜" flat washers (9 required)

⅜" nut

⅜" all-thread rod 5½" long

SANDING THE WHEELS

THE HEAVY HAULIN' LOADER

continued

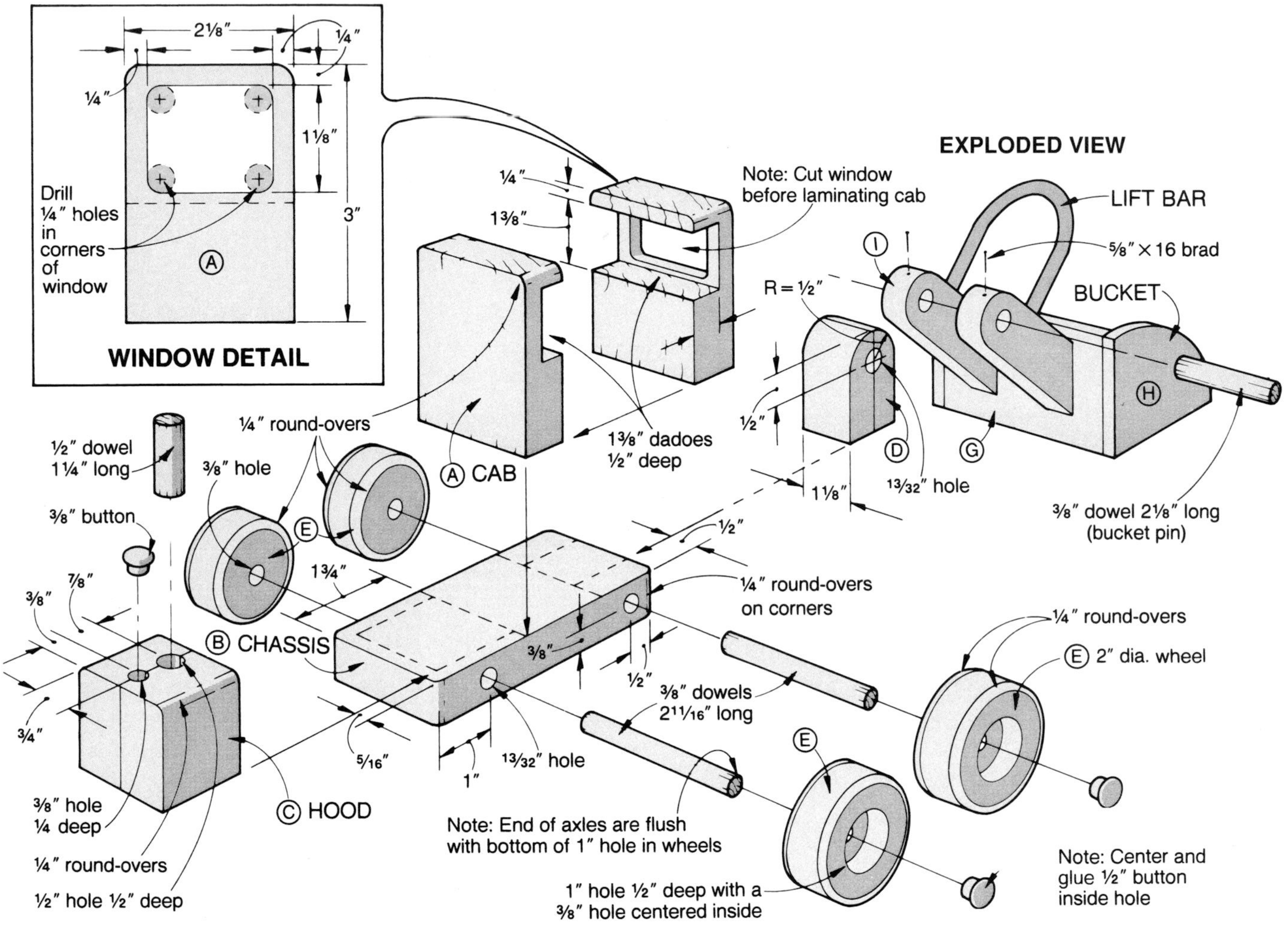
WINDOW DETAIL
2⅛"
¼"
¼"
1⅛"
3"
Drill ¼" holes in corners of window
Ⓐ
EXPLODED VIEW
Note: Cut window before laminating cab
LIFT BAR
⅝" × 16 brad
BUCKET
R = ½"
Ⓘ
¼"
1⅜"
¼" round-overs
Ⓐ CAB
1⅜" dadoes ½" deep
½"
1⅛"
Ⓓ
Ⓖ
Ⓗ
13/32" hole
⅜" dowel 2⅛" long (bucket pin)
½" dowel 1¼" long
⅜" hole
⅜" button
Ⓔ
1¾"
⅞"
⅜"
Ⓑ CHASSIS
½"
¼" round-overs on corners
¼" round-overs
Ⓔ 2" dia. wheel
⅜"
½"
⅜" dowels 2¹¹⁄₁₆" long
¾"
5/16"
1"
13/32" hole
Ⓔ
⅜" hole ¼ deep
Ⓒ HOOD
¼" round-overs
½" hole ½" deep
Note: End of axles are flush with bottom of 1" hole in wheels
1" hole ½" deep with a ⅜" hole centered inside
Note: Center and glue ½" button inside hole

Bill of Materials					
Parts	Finished Size*			Mat.	Qty.
	T	W	L		
A cab	1½"	2⅛"	3"	LP	1
B chassis	¾"	2⅛"	4¼"	P	1
C hood	1½"	1½"	1½"	LP	1
D support	1"	1⅛"	1⅝"	LP	1
E* wheels	¾"	2" dia.		P	4
BUCKET ASSEMBLY					
F bottom	¼"	2"	3"	P	1
G back	¼"	2¼"	3"	P	1
H ends	¼"	2¼"	2¼"	P	2
I arms	½"	1"	2⅝"	P	2

*Initially cut parts marked with an * oversized. Then, trim each to finished size according to the how-to instructions.

Material Key: LP–laminated pine, P–pine
Supplies: ⅜" dowel stock, ½" dowel stock, ⅜" wood button, ½" wood buttons, ⅜" all-thread rod 5½" long with nuts and washers for sanding arbor, ¼X1½" U-bolt, #4X½" flathead wood screws, ⅝"X16 brads, clear finish.

cab to the chassis and support, and then add the hood.

Time to add some wheels

1. To make four wheels (E), cut a piece of ¾"-thick pine to 4X14". Starting 3" from one end, mark four centerpoints 3" apart.

2. With a compass, mark a 2"-diameter circle (1" radius) at each marked centerpoint.

3. Chuck a 1" Forstner bit into your drill press. Center the bit over each marked centerpoint, and bore a ½"-deep hole as shown in the photo on *page 33, left*. (We used the stop on our drill press to ensure uniform depth.)

4. Chuck a circle cutter into your drill press. Turn the cutter blade with the pointed end on the inside to cut a perfect wheel. Raise the blade ⅜" higher than the bottom of the pilot bit. Center the pilot bit over the depression left by the Forstner bit in each 1" hole, and slowly—about 250 to 500 rpm—cut the wheels to shape as shown in the photo on *page 33, right*.

5. Remove the circle cutter, and chuck a ⅜" twist drill bit into your drill press. Secure a wheel in a handscrew clamp, and enlarge the ¼" pilot (axle) hole to ⅜". Repeat for each wheel.

6. Cut a piece of ⅜" all-thread rod to 5½" long. Chuck it into your drill press. Attach two wheels at a time to the threaded rod where shown in the drawing on *page 33, bottom*. With the drill press running at about 750 rpm, hand-sand a ¼" round-over on each wheel where shown in the drawing. (We found sanding the round-overs safer than trying to rout them on a router table.)

Next, assemble the bucket

1. Cut the bucket bottom (F), back (G), and ends (H) to size and shape from ¼" stock. Sand a ⅛" chamfer along the top front edge of the bucket bottom.

2. From ½" stock, cut the arms (I) to size, mitering the front ends at 45°. See the drawings *below right* for reference and the Bill of Materials for sizes.

3. Mark the centerpoints, and drill a ¼" hole ½" deep in each arm for the lift-bar U-bolt and a ⅜" hole through each bucket arm.

4. Sand the pieces. Then, with the edges and ends flush, glue and clamp the bucket parts (F, G, H).

5. Using a hacksaw, trim the ends of a 1½" U-bolt so only ½" of threaded portion remains on each end (see the Bucket Assembly drawing for specifics).

6. Set the arms on a flat surface, and epoxy the threaded ends of the U-bolt into the ¼" holes in the arms, checking that the arms are parallel to each other and that the mitered front ends remain flush. (You want the bucket support to fit easily between the arms.)

7. Hold the arm assembly against the back of the bucket assembly, and trace the arms outlines onto the bucket back. Drill four ⁷⁄₆₄" holes through the back and ⁵⁄₆₄" pilot holes into the arms. Screw the arms to the bucket back.

8. Cut a ⅜" dowel to 2⅛" long for the bucket pin. Position the arms on both sides of the bucket support and slide the dowel pin in place. Snip off the head of a ⅝"×16 brad and chuck it into your portable drill. Drill a pilot hole through each arm and into the dowel pin. Drive a ⅝"×16 brad through each pilot hole to secure the arms to the bucket pin.

Mount the wheels, and move some gravel

1. Cut the axles to length from ⅜" dowel stock as dimensioned on the Exploded View drawing.

2. Glue one wheel onto each dowel axle so that the end of the dowel is flush with the inside of the counterbore. After the glue dries, slide the axle through the axle hole and glue another wheel to the end of the axle dowel, leaving enough free play so the wheels turn easily.

3. To add the hubcaps, set the loader on its side. Place a drop of glue on the ends of the axle dowels, and glue a ½" wood button to the end of the dowel. After the glue dries, flip over the assembly and repeat for the other hubcaps.

4. Add the radiator cap and smokestack. Mask the U-bolt and apply the finish.

Project Tool List
Tablesaw
   Dado blade or dado set
Scrollsaw
Bandsaw
Drill
Drill press
   Circle cutter
   Bits: ⁵⁄₆₄", ⁷⁄₆₄", ¼", ½", ⅜", ¹³⁄₃₂", 1"
Finishing sander

Note: We built the project using the tools listed. You may be able to substitute other tools or equipment for listed items you don't have. Additional common tools and clamps may be required to complete the project.

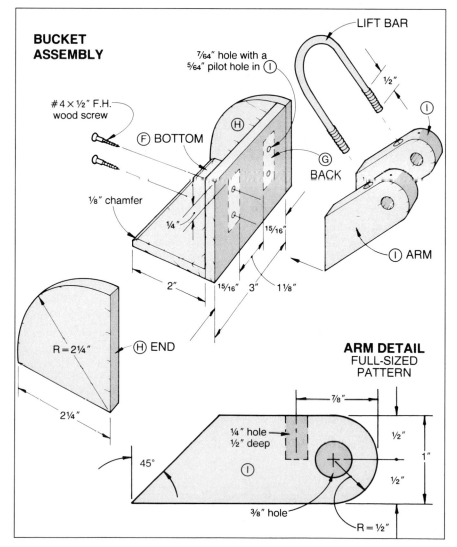

BUCKET ASSEMBLY

LIFT BAR

⁷⁄₆₄" hole with a ⁵⁄₆₄" pilot hole in (I)

½"

(I)

#4 × ½" F.H. wood screw

(F) BOTTOM

(H)

(G) BACK

⅛" chamfer

¼"

15/16"

(I) ARM

2"

15/16" 3" 1⅛"

R = 2¼"

(H) END

2¼"

ARM DETAIL
FULL-SIZED PATTERN

⅞"

¼" hole ½" deep

½"

1"

45°

(I)

½"

⅜" hole

R = ½"

35

ROUGH 'N' READY WRECKER

Every now and then, even the sturdiest toy vehicle "breaks down" somewhere and needs to go to the "shop" for repairs. When that happens at your house, we've got the truck your child needs to get the hauling job done. For heavy loads, simply have him lock the boom's lift bar in the up position—just like the real McCoy—and off he'll go.

Note: You'll need some thin stock for this project. You can either plane or resaw thicker stock to the sizes in the Bill of Materials.

Laminate the cab

1. Cut a piece of ¾" pine to 2" wide by 12" long for the cab (A).

2. Measuring 1" from each end of the pine stock, mark the location for a 1⅜" dado. Cut the

marked dadoes ½" deep where shown on the *opposite page.*

3. Crosscut the pine into two equal lengths. Mark the windshield location on one piece where shown on the Windshield detail accompanying the Tractor drawing. Align the top of the windshield flush with the top of the dado. Now drill four ¼" holes inside the marked square. Cut the opening to shape with a scrollsaw or coping saw. Sand or file the edges of the opening.

4. Apply glue to the mating surfaces of cab parts (A), align the dadoes, and clamp. Remove excess glue before it dries.

5. Trim the top and bottom of the cab lamination to length where shown on the Windshield detail.

Now, cut the body parts

1. Cut the hood (B), chassis (C), and bed (D), to the sizes listed in

Bill of Materials

Part	Finished Size*			Mat.	Qty.
	T	W	L		
A* cab	1½"	2"	3"	LP	1
B hood	¾"	2"	1½"	P	1
C chassis	¾"	2"	6¾"	P	1
D bed	¾"	¾"	4¼"	P	1
E boom	¾"	1¾"	5⅛"	P	1
F lift bar	¼"	½"	3⅝"	B	1
G hook	¼"	1"	1⅛"	B	1
H *inner wheels	¾"	2" dia.		P	4
I *outer wheels	¾"	2" dia.		P	6

*Initially cut parts marked with an * oversized. Then, trim each to finished size according to the how-to instructions.
Material key: LP–laminated pine, P–pine, B–Birch
Supplies: #8 finish nails, 10—⅜" flat washers, mason's line or ¹⁄₁₆"-dia. cord, ⅜" dowel stock, ½" dowel stock, 7—½" hood buttons, ⅜" all-thread rod 5½" long with nuts and washers for sanding arbor, ½" wooden buttons, clear finish.

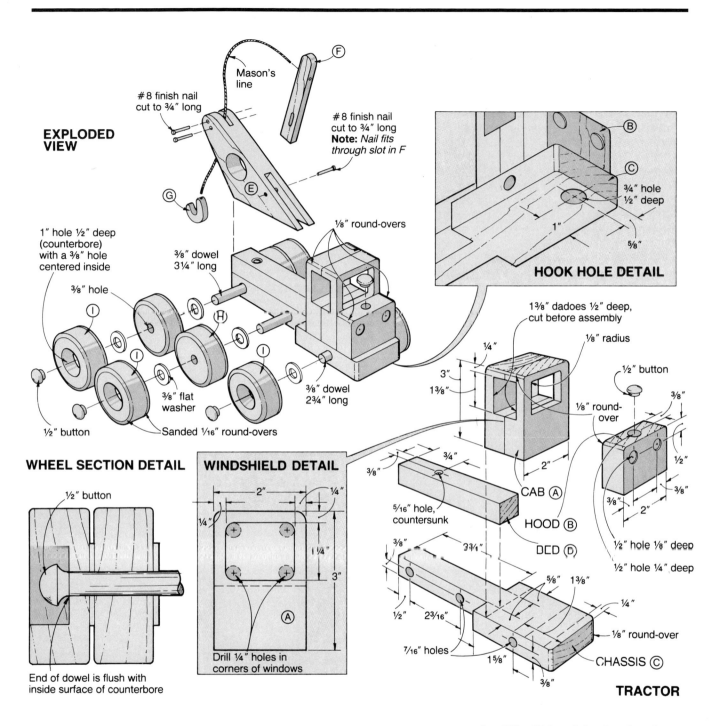

EXPLODED VIEW

Mason's line

#8 finish nail cut to ¾" long

#8 finish nail cut to ¾" long
Note: *Nail fits through slot in F*

F

G

E

1" hole ½" deep (counterbore) with a ⅜" hole centered inside

⅜" dowel 3¼" long

⅛" round-overs

⅜" hole

1

H

⅜" flat washer

½" button

⅜" dowel 2¾" long

Sanded ¹⁄₁₆" round-overs

½" button

HOOK HOLE DETAIL

B

C

¾" hole ½" deep

1"

⅝"

1⅜" dadoes ½" deep, cut before assembly

⅛" radius

½" button

¼"

3"

1⅜"

⅛" round-over

⅛" round-over

2"

CAB Ⓐ

HOOD Ⓑ

⅜"

½"

⅜"

⅜"

2"

½" hole ⅛" deep

½" hole ¼" deep

WHEEL SECTION DETAIL

½" button

End of dowel is flush with inside surface of counterbore

WINDSHIELD DETAIL

2"

¼"

¼"

1¼"

3"

Ⓐ

Drill ¼" holes in corners of windows

¾"

⅜"

⁵⁄₁₆" hole, countersunk

BED Ⓓ

⅜"

3¾"

½"

2³⁄₁₆"

⁷⁄₁₆" holes

1⅝"

⅝"

1⅜"

¼"

⅛" round-over

CHASSIS Ⓒ

⅜"

TRACTOR

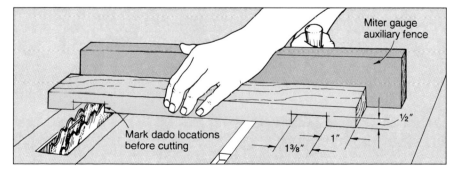

Miter gauge auxiliary fence

Mark dado locations before cutting

½"

1"

1⅜"

the Bill of Materials. Cut the chassis to the shape shown on the Tractor drawing.

2. Sand ⅛" round-overs on the hood, cab, and chassis where shown on the Tractor drawing.

3. Mark all the hole centerpoints on the hood, chassis, and bed. One at a time, support each piece with a handscrew clamp, and drill the holes (we used a drill press) to the sizes listed on the Tractor drawing.

continued

ROUGH 'N' READY WRECKER
continued

Don't forget to drill a ¾" hole ½" deep on the bottom front of your other toys where shown in the Hook Hole detail accompanying the Exploded View drawing. The hole allows the wrecker hook (G) to fit into it for towing.

4. With the bottom and edges of the cab and hood flush, glue and clamp them together. Recessing the hood ¼" from the front end of the chassis to form the bumper, glue and clamp the cab assembly to the chassis. Later, glue and clamp the bed on top of the chassis and against the back of the cab. Sand smooth, and glue a ½" button into the radiator cap hole.

Add the boom and lift bar

1. From ¾" pine, cut a block 1¾x5⅛" long for the boom (E).

2. Using carbon paper, transfer the boom outline, hole centerpoints, and ⅛" and ¼" slot locations to the boom blank.

3. Drill the holes to the sizes stated on the Boom drawing.

4. With a bandsaw, cut the slots to size. (You also could use a push block, and cut the slots on the tablesaw.) Cut the boom to shape.

5. Glue the boom to the bed where shown on the Section View drawing.

6. Using carbon paper and the full-sized patterns, transfer the lift bar (F) and the hook (G) outlines, as well as the hole and slot locations for each to ¼" birch stock. Cut the two parts to shape.

7. Form the slot in the lift bar where marked. Using a handscrew clamp to hold the parts steady, drill a ¹⁄₁₆" hole through the hook and lift bar where marked. Then, drill the ⅛" counterbores. These holes will hide the boom-line knots later.

8. Snip three #8 finish nails to ¾" long. Position the lift bar in the boom slot. Press the top two nails into the ³⁄₃₂" holes in the boom. (We used a drop of instant glue in each hole to secure the nails.) Align the

slot in the lift bar with the lower ³⁄₃₂" hole in the boom, and press the bottom nail into position, trapping the lift bar in the boom slot.

9. Cut a piece of cord (we used mason's line) to about 7" long. Tie a knot on one end and thread the other end through the hole in the lift bar, pulling the knot into the counter-bore. Pass the line between the nails in the boom, and thread it through the hole in the hook. Now, tie a knot on this end and tug the line to draw the knot into the hook's ⅛" hole.

Next up, the wheels

1. To make 10 wheels (H, I), cut a piece of ¾"-thick pine to 4x36". Starting 3" from one end, mark 10 centerpoints 3" apart.

2. With a compass, mark a 2"-diameter circle (1" radius) at each marked centerpoint.

3. Chuck a 1" Forstner bit into your drill press. Attach a scrap work surface to your drill-press table. As shown in the photo *above right,* center the bit over a marked centerpoint, and bore a ½"-deep hole in six of the marked circles. (We used the stop on our drill press to ensure a uniform depth.)

4. Chuck a circle cutter into your drill press. Using the drawing at *right* for reference, turn the cutter blade so the pointed end is on the inside to cut a perfect wheel. Adjust the circle-cutter arm to cut the correct diameter.

5. Raise the cutter blade ⅝" higher than the bottom of the pilot bit. Center the pilot bit over the depression left by the Forstner bit in each 1" hole or over the marked centerpoint on the four marked circles, and slowly cut the 10 wheels to shape as shown in the photo at *right.*

6. Remove the circle cutter, and chuck a ⅜" twist drill bit into your drill press. Secure a wheel in a small handscrew clamp, and enlarge the ¼" pilot hole to ⅜". Repeat for each wheel.

Mark the wheel centerpoints and radii, and use a 1" Forstner bit to drill holes ½" deep for each wheel.

7. Cut a piece of ⅜" all-thread rod to 5½" long, and chuck it into your drill press. Then, using nuts and washers, attach a pair of wheels to the work arbor where shown in the drawing *opposite.* With the drill press running at about 750 rpm, hand-sand a ⅛" round-over on the wheels where shown on the drawing. (We found sanding the round-overs safer and easier than trying to rout them on a router table.)

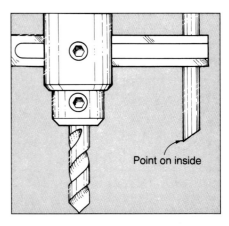

Point on inside

Center the circle-cutter pilot bit over the Forstner-bit depression, and cut the outside of the wheels to shape.

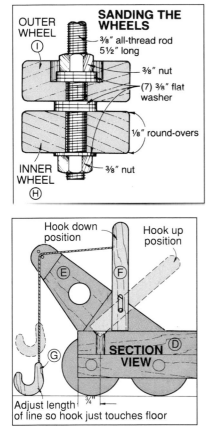

SANDING THE WHEELS

OUTER WHEEL Ⓘ

⅜" all-thread rod 5½" long

⅜" nut

(7) ⅜" flat washer

⅛" round-overs

INNER WHEEL Ⓗ

⅜" nut

Hook down position

Hook up position

Ⓔ   Ⓕ

SECTION VIEW   Ⓓ

Ⓖ

Adjust length of line so hook just touches floor

¾"

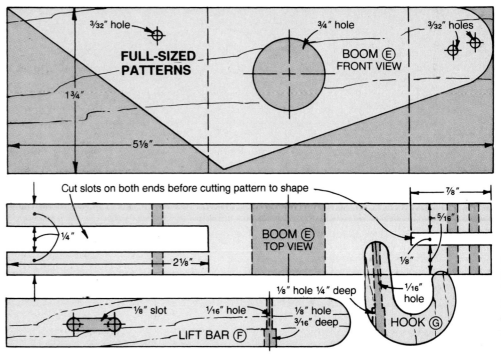

FULL-SIZED PATTERNS

³⁄₃₂" hole

¾" hole

BOOM Ⓔ FRONT VIEW

³⁄₃₂" holes

1¾"

5⅛"

Cut slots on both ends before cutting pattern to shape

¼"

2⅛"

BOOM Ⓔ TOP VIEW

⅞"

⁵⁄₁₆"

⅛"

HOOK Ⓖ

⅛" slot

¹⁄₁₆" hole

⅛" hole ¼" deep

⅛" hole ³⁄₁₆" deep

¹⁄₁₆" hole

LIFT BAR Ⓕ

Mount the wheels

1. Cut two ⅜" axles to 3¼" long and one to 2¾" long.

2. Glue one wheel onto each dowel axle so the end of the dowel is flush with the inside of the counterbore where shown on the Wheel Section detail. After the glue dries, place ⅜" flat washers on the axles next to the glued wheels. Slide the front axle through the front-axle hole, and add a washer onto the protruding axle end. Glue on the remaining wheel, leaving enough free play so the wheels turn easily. Repeat the process with the back axles, adding an inside wheel and washer on each side of the chassis.

3. To add the hub caps, set the wrecker on its side. Place a drop of glue on the ends of the axle dowels, and glue a ½" button on the end of the dowel. After the glue dries, flip over the assembly and repeat for the other hub caps.

4. Apply a clear finish to all the parts (for a durable finish, we used polyurethane).

Project Tool List
Tablesaw
  Dado blade or dado set
Scrollsaw
Drill press
  Circle cutter
  Bits: ¹⁄₁₆", ³⁄₃₂", ⅛", ¼", ⁵⁄₁₆", ⅜", ⁷⁄₁₆", ½", ¾", 1"
Finishing sander

Note: We built the project using the tools listed. You may be able to substitute other tools or equipment for listed items you don't have. Additional common tools and clamps may be required to complete the project.

RUBBER-BAND DRAGSTER

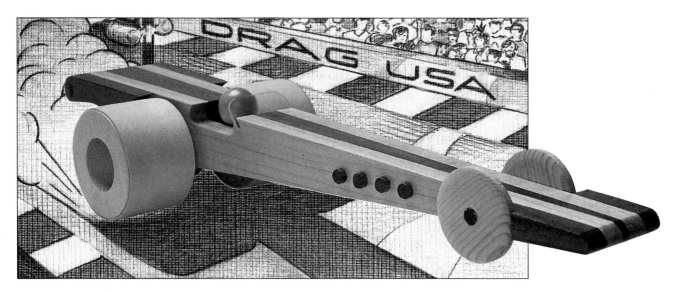

Zoom into the winner's circle with this exciting action toy designed for race-car buffs of all ages. Rubber-band powered, our striped dragster digs in from the start, thanks to two 1½"-wide rubber-band treads on the slick-like rear wheels. For the best results, though, race the cars on smooth surfaces such as vinyl, wood, or concrete flooring.

Let's make the body

1. Rip and crosscut two ¾"-thick pieces of walnut to 1¾ x14" for parts A, C, and D, and two ¾"-thick pieces of maple to 1¾ x14" for the B parts. (See the Cutting Diagram *opposite*.)

2. Using double-faced tape, attach a 1½ x1½ x14" piece of scrap to the face of one of the ¾"-thick walnut pieces. Align the bottom edges of the two pieces flush. To

make the tapered body part A (see the Top View drawing on *page 43*), mark ⅛" in from one corner on the top edge of the walnut piece. Scribe a line from this point along the length of the edge to the opposing diagonal corner. Now, bandsaw just outside the line as shown in drawing A, *opposite*. Sand the piece to the line. (We used a stationary belt sander as shown in drawing B, holding the piece with

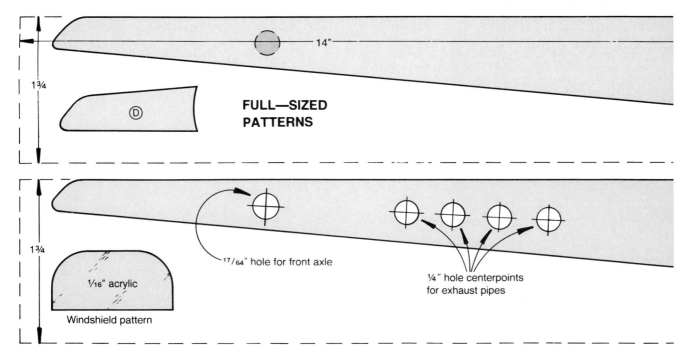

14"

1¾

Ⓓ

FULL—SIZED PATTERNS

1¾

1/16" acrylic

Windshield pattern

¹⁷/₆₄" hole for front axle

¼" hole centerpoints for exhaust pipes

the scrap.) Separate the scrap from the tapered walnut piece.

3. Using the same technique, and the dimensions on the Wedge Block drawing on *page 42*, cut a second tapered piece from scrap. Set it aside until needed later.

Cutting Diagram

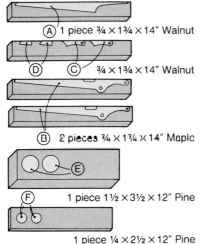

Ⓐ 1 piece ¾ × 1¾ × 14″ Walnut

Ⓓ   Ⓒ   ¾ × 1¾ × 14″ Walnut

Ⓑ 2 pieces ¾ × 1¾ × 14″ Maple

Ⓔ   1 piece 1½ × 3½ × 12″ Pine

Ⓕ   1 piece ¼ × 2½ × 12″ Pine

4. Now, resaw or plane the second ¾"-thick piece of walnut and the two ¾"-thick maple pieces to ⅜".

5. Photocopy the full-sized patterns for parts A, B, C, D, and windshield shown *opposite* and *below*. Cut along the top edges of each pattern and separate them. Using spray adhesive, adhere pattern A to the side of the tapered piece of walnut, aligning the pattern's top with the top of the piece, and locating the dragster's front on the narrow end of the piece. Stick the two maple pieces together with double-faced tape, and adhere pattern B to the side of one piece. Next, cut the remaining piece of ⅜"-thick walnut into two equal lengths, and stack them, again, using double-faced tape. Apply patterns C and D to the top piece.

6. Chuck a ¼" brad-point bit in your drill press and bore the exhaust pipe holes shown on the pattern through the joined maple

pieces. See drawing C. (We backed the pieces with scrap to prevent splintering.) Change bits and drill the ¹⁷⁄₆₄" holes through the maple pieces for the front axle and rubber-band bar. Also, drill the hole in part C. Change bits again and drill the ²⁵⁄₆₄" rear axle hole through the maple pieces. (Drilling the axle holes now allows for precise alignment, but you will need to redrill the front axle hole again, once you glue-join body parts A and B.)

7. Now, cut the body parts to shape as shown in drawing D, and sand the edges smooth. (We used a drum sander and a stationary belt sander.) Remove the patterns from parts A, C, and D, and separate all tape-joined parts. (We removed adhesive residue with lacquer thinner.)

8. Clamp a scrap wood block to the edge of your workbench. Next, apply glue (we applied a moderate *continued*

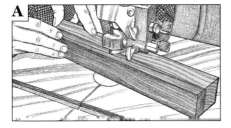

A

B

C

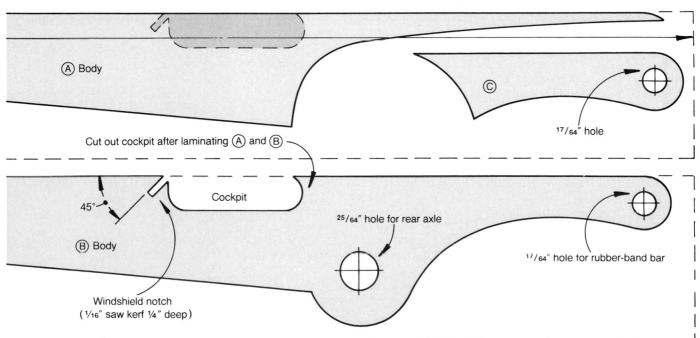

Ⓐ Body

Ⓒ

¹⁷⁄₆₄" hole

Cut out cockpit after laminating Ⓐ and Ⓑ

45°

Cockpit

²⁵⁄₆₄" hole for rear axle

¹⁷⁄₆₄" hole for rubber-band bar

Ⓑ Body

Windshield notch
(¹⁄₁₆" saw kerf ¼" deep)

RUBBER-BAND DRAGSTER

continued

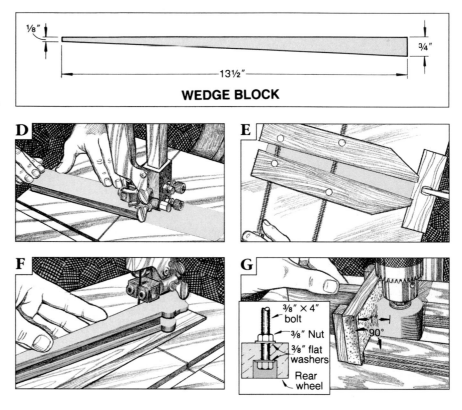

amount of yellow woodworker's glue) to both sides of part A. Using the Top View drawing as a guide, position part A between the two Bs. Place this assembly on your workbench, top side down. With one end against the block, align the pieces, and clamp the assembly as shown in drawing E. (We placed a sheet of waxed paper under the car to keep glue off the benchtop.)

9. After the glue dries, remove the clamp. Next, tape one side of the partially assembled body to the tapered scrap piece with double-faced tape. Locate the wide end of the taper beneath the narrow end of the car. This should level the side of the body with the work surface. Saw out the cockpit and the windshield notch. (We used a bandsaw as shown in drawing F.) Next, drill the ¹⁷⁄₆₄" front axle hole.

10. Peel off the tapered scrap piece, remove the patterns, and clean off any remaining adhesive. Apply glue to the joining surfaces of trim parts C, align them on the front of the body, and clamp them in place using the Top View drawing as a guide. Next, cut a 2¼"-long ¼" dowel. Glue parts D to the car body where shown on the Top View drawing. Insert the ¼" dowel through the holes in parts B and C to help align them. Clamp parts D until the glue dries. Finally, remove the clamps and sand the body.

Now, make the wheels

1. Chuck a ⅜" brad-point (or twist) bit in your drill press. Measure 4" in from each end of a 12"-long 2×4 and strike lines at these locations across the width. Find the center of these lines and scribe a 2"-diameter-circle on each with a compass. Place the 2×4 on an equally long piece of scrap, and clamp both to your drill press table, centering the bit over one of the circle centerpoints. Drill through the 2×4. Next, change to a

1" Forstner bit and drill a hole ¾" deep. If you use a spade bit, drill the 1" hole, and then the ⅜" hole. Repeat these operations for the other circle.

2. Saw the rear wheels (E) to shape on a bandsaw, cutting just outside the line. Thread a ⅜" bolt through the rear wheels as shown in the insert detail of drawing G, *above right,* and chuck it into your drill press. Now, sand the wheels to the finished diameter. (We used the sanding jig shown in drawing G, starting with 60-grit aluminum oxide cloth. A support holds the block at 90°. Two parallel wood strips—one on each side of the wheel—extend exactly 1" beyond the wheel's centerpoint.)

3. To make the front wheels (F), set a circle cutter with a ¼" drill bit to cut a 1½"-diameter circle, and mount it in your drill press. Cut a ¾×2½×12" piece of pine, and

resaw or plane it to ¼" thickness. Measure 4" in from each end and strike lines across the width. Place the wood on a piece of scrap, and clamp both to your drill-press table, centering the circle cutter over one of the two lines. Now, cut one wheel. Reposition the piece with the other line centered under the circle cutter. Cut out the second wheel as shown in drawing H, *opposite.*

4. Mount a front wheel to your drill press, this time using a ¼" bolt, washers, and nut. Using a handheld sanding block, round over the wheel's edges as shown in drawing I. Round over the other wheel.

You're nearing the finish line

1. Cut eight pieces of ¼" walnut dowel to ⁷⁄₁₆" long. Add glue to one end and insert the dowels in the exhaust pipe holes so they extend ¹⁄₁₆". Next, cut one piece of ¼"

TOP VIEW

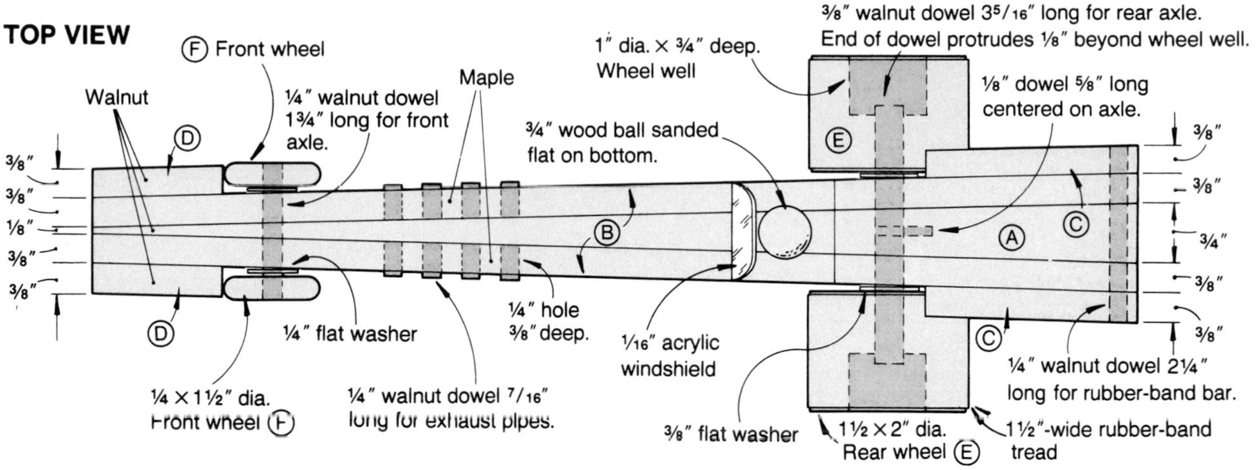

F Front wheel
Walnut
D
¼" walnut dowel 1¾" long for front axle.
Maple
1" dia. × ¾" deep. Wheel well
3/8" walnut dowel 3 5/16" long for rear axle. End of dowel protrudes ⅛" beyond wheel well.
⅛" dowel ⅝" long centered on axle.
¾" wood ball sanded flat on bottom.
E
B
A
C
⅜"
⅜"
⅛"
⅜"
⅜"
⅜"
⅜"
¾"
⅜"
⅜"
¼" hole ⅜" deep.
1/16" acrylic windshield
¼" flat washer
¼ × 1½" dia. Front wheel F
¼" walnut dowel 7/16" long for exhaust pipes.
⅜" flat washer
1½ × 2" dia. Rear wheel E
1½"-wide rubber-band tread
¼" walnut dowel 2¼" long for rubber-band bar.

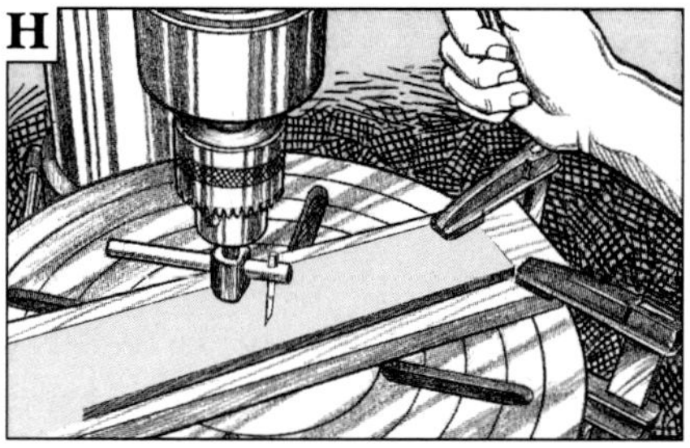
H

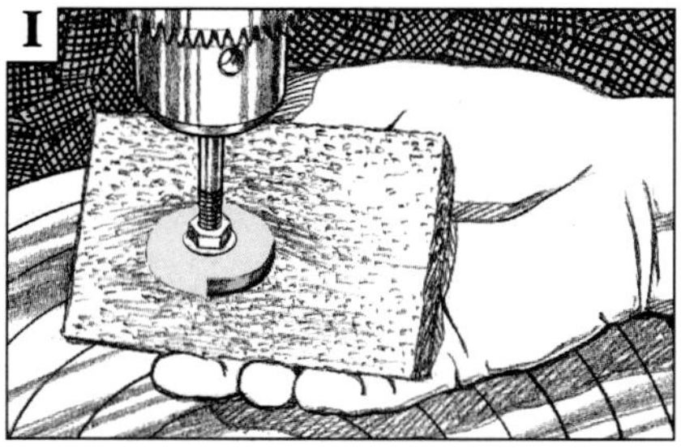
I

Bill of Materials

Part	Finished Size* T	W	L	Mat.	Qty.
A	¾"	1¾"	14"	W	1
B	¾"	1¾"	14"	M	2
C	¾"	1¾"	3"	W	2
D	⅜"	1¾"	2"	W	2
E*	1½"	2" dia.		P	2
F*	¼"	1½" dia.		P	2

*Parts marked with an * are listed in finished size.

Material Key: W–walnut, M–maple, P–pine
Supplies: 1—¾"-diameter maple wood ball; 1—⅛" birch dowel; 1—¼" walnut dowel; 1—⅜" walnut dowel; 1/16"-thick acrylic; 2—¼" and ⅜" flat washers; ¼x3½" rubber band.

walnut dowel to 1¾" for the front axle. Now, cut one piece of ⅜" walnut dowel to 3 5/16" for the rear axle, and drill a 1/16" hole through the center of it. Finally, cut one piece of ⅛" dowel to ⅝" long.

2. Sand a flat spot on a ¾" wood ball (available at craft supply stores), and glue it in the cockpit where shown on the Top View drawing.

3. Apply a finish of your choice to the body and wheels. (We sprayed on four coats of clear gloss lacquer, sanding lightly between applications with 220-grit sandpaper.)

4. Insert the front axle through the body, add ¼" flat washers, and glue on the front wheels. (We lubricated both axles with paste wax before adding them to the car.)

5. Insert the rear axle through the body, and glue in the ⅛" dowel pin. Next, add the ⅜" flat washers, and then glue on the wheels as shown in the Top View drawing.

6. Using the windshield pattern (*page 40*), cut a piece of 1/16" thick clear acrylic to shape. (We used a scroll-saw.) Apply glue in the band-sawed slot, and then insert the windshield in the slot.

7. Slip the rubber-band treads on the rear wheels (see the Buying Guide for a source). Loop or tie one end of a ¼ x3½" rubber band around the rear bar. To operate the car, loop the other end of the rubber band onto the ⅛" pin on the rear axle, turn the wheels clockwise or backwards, set the dragster on a smooth surface, and let it roll!

Buying Guide

- **Traction rubber bands.** 1½"-wide rubber bands, catalog no. 7338. For current prices, contact Meisel Hardware Specialties, P.O. Box 70, Mound, MN 55364-0700 or call 800-441-9870.

Project Tool List

Tablesaw
Bandsaw
Scrollsaw
Belt sander
Drill press
  Sanding drum
  Circle cutter
  Bits: ⅛", ¼", 17/64", ⅜", 25/64", 1"
Finishing sander

Note: *We built the project using the tools listed. You may be able to substitute other tools or equipment for listed items you don't have. Additional common tools and clamps may be required to complete the project.*

RED-HOT FIRE TRUCK

It was love at first sight when we spotted Tom Lewis's fire truck not long ago at a California crafts show. Tom tells us that because kids can take apart and then reassemble this fire truck easily, they'll play with it day after day.

Let's begin with the chassis

1. Saw two pieces of ¾" pine to 2½ x7½" for the chassis (A). See our Cutting diagram *opposite*. Stack the two pieces face to face with double-faced tape. The top piece becomes a drilling template.

2. Using the dimensions on the Chassis drawing, lay out the six hole centerpoints on the *face* of the top piece. Drill these ¼" holes through the template and ⅜" deep into the chassis. (We used our drill press.) Now, separate the two pieces and lay aside the template.

3. Round over the corners of the chassis as shown on the Chassis drawing. (We used our disc sander.) Finish-sand the piece.

4. Cut six 1⅜" lengths of ¼" dowel and chamfer one end on each. Place a drop of glue (we used yellow woodworker's glue) in one of the holes you just drilled, and insert a dowel into that hole, chamfered end up. Now, glue the remaining dowels in the other five holes.

5. Select toy axle pegs to fit the hole of your wood wheels. (Our wheels had a ¼" hole requiring ⁷⁄₃₂"-diameter axle pegs. We found peg sizes can vary depending on supplier, so drill a hole in scrap first to check the fit of your axle pegs: They should fit snugly. If they don't, select a different bit.) When you're satisfied with the fit, lay out, and then drill the four axle holes

¾" deep in the *edges* of the chassis where shown on the Chassis drawing. (We clamped the piece on edge in a handscrew clamp.)

Now, move on to the other body parts

1. From ¾" pine, rip and cross-cut three 2" squares for the hood (B) block. Resaw one of the pieces to ½" thick. Next, glue the three pieces together, sandwiching the ½"-thick piece in the center as shown in the Hood detail. (When clamping, we used scrap-wood pads between the clamp and hood pieces to prevent the clamps from denting the soft pine.)

2. Using the dimensions on the Hood detail, mark the centerpoint for the radiator-cap hole on the top of the block. Drill the ⁷⁄₃₂" hole 1" deep and at an angle 30° from perpendicular. (We placed a shim under the block to hold it at approximately this angle while drilling the hole on our drill press.)

3. Copy the four patterns found on *page 47*. (We made photocopies.) Adhere the hood pattern to the *side* of the hood block. (We used spray adhesive.) Next, using your tablesaw, cut the four ⅛"-wide kerfs ¾" deep in the hood front where shown on the Hood detail. Turn the block so the pattern

Bill of Materials				
Part	**Finished Size**		**Mat.**	**Qty.**
	T	**W**	**L**		
A chassis	¾"	2½"	7½"	P	2
B hood	2"	2"	1¾"	LP	1
C fenders	¾"	⅞"	1⅝"	P	2
D cab	1½"	3½"	3"	LP	1
E seat	1½"	3"	1½"	LP	1
F roof	¼"	3½"	2½"	P	1
G ladder rack	¾"	3½"	3¾"	P	1
H ladder stringer	½"	½"	5"	P	6

Material Key: LP—laminated pine, P—pine
Supplies: ¼" dowel stock, 4—⅝ X2" wheels, 4 —¼" flat washers, 9—⁷⁄₃₂ X ⅛" toy axle pegs, paint and finish.

CHASSIS

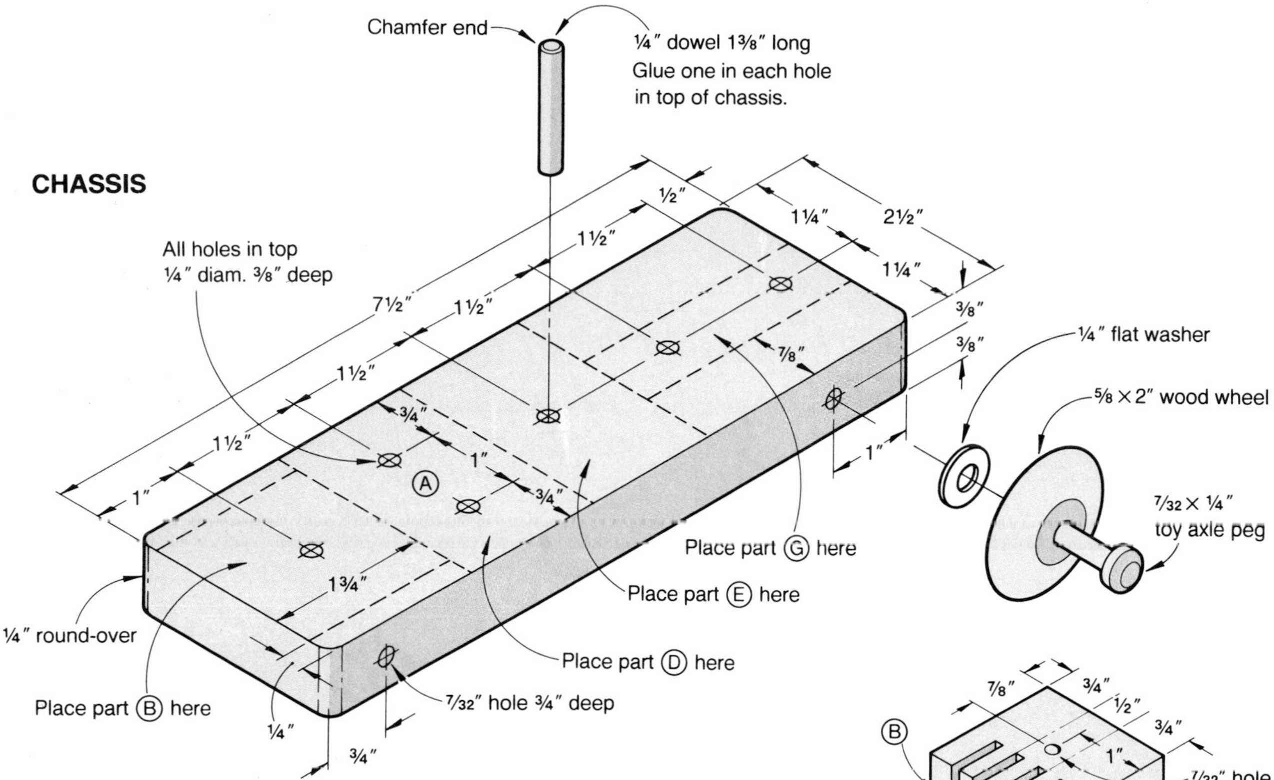

Chamfer end
¼" dowel 1⅜" long
Glue one in each hole
in top of chassis.
All holes in top
¼" diam. ⅜" deep
½"
1½"
1¼"
2½"
1¼"
7½"
1½"
⅜"
⅜"
⅞"
1½"
¾"
1½"
1"
1"
1"
¾"
1¾"
A
¼" round-over
Place part B here
¼"
¾"
7/32" hole ¾" deep
Place part D here
Place part E here
Place part G here
¼" flat washer
⅝ × 2" wood wheel
7/32 × ¼"
toy axle peg

CUTTING DIAGRAM

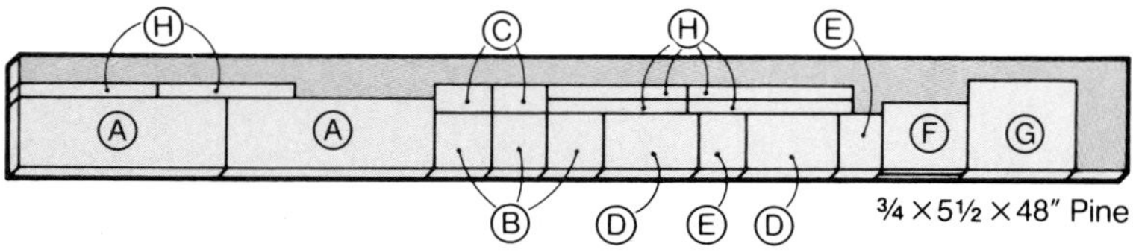

H
C
H
E
A
A
F
G
B
D
E
D
¾ × 5½ × 48" Pine

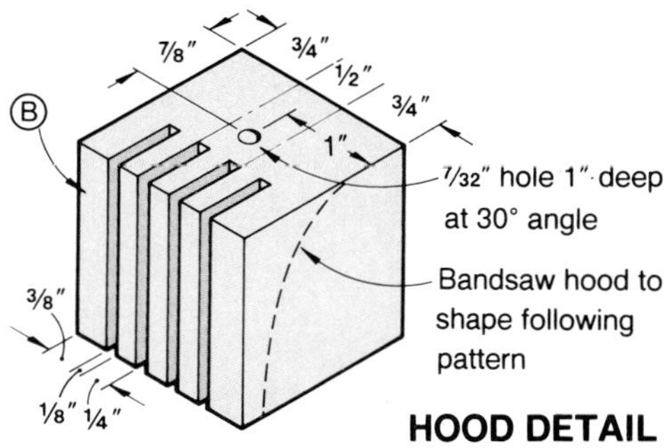

B
⅞"
¾"
½"
¾"
1"
7/32" hole 1" deep
at 30° angle
Bandsaw hood to
shape following
pattern
⅜"
⅛"
¼"

HOOD DETAIL

side faces up. Bandsaw the hood to shape. (We sawed just outside of the pattern line, and then sanded to the line using our disc sander.)

4. For the front fenders (C), first rip and crosscut two pieces of ¾" stock to 1X2". Using double-faced tape, stack the two pieces together. Next, adhere the Fender pattern to the top piece. Bandsaw or scrollsaw the fenders to shape. Now, separate the parts, remove the tape, and then glue and clamp them to the hood where shown on the Exploded View on *page 46.*

5. From ¾" pine, rip and crosscut two pieces to 3½ X5". Glue them together face to face, aligning the edges and ends, and clamp. Remove the clamps from this blank after the glue dries.

6. Set the rip fence on your tablesaw 1⅛" from the inside of the saw blade. Angle the blade 20° from perpendicular, and rip the bevel along one end of the piece as shown *right.* From this blank, crosscut a 3" length (include the beveled end) for the cab (D). Next, crosscut a 1½" length from the piece for the passenger seat (E). Bore a ¾" hole ⅜" deep in the center of the seat. (We used a Forstner bit.)

7. Rip and crosscut a piece of ¾" pine to 3X4", and then resaw and sand this piece to ¼" thick. (We resawed it on our bandsaw.) Adhere the Roof (F) pattern to the piece, and saw it to shape. Remove your pattern. Now, glue the roof to the top of the cab as shown in the Cab detail on the Exploded View drawing on *page 46.*

8. To make the ladder rack (G), rip and crosscut a piece of ¾" pine to 4X4". Adhere the ladder rack pattern to the side of the piece, aligning it along two adjacent sides. Drill the three holes through

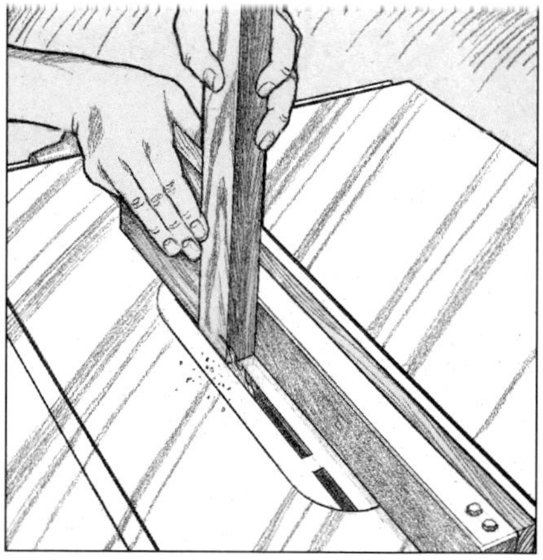

the piece where marked on the pattern. (We backed the part with scrap when drilling to prevent splintering the edges.) Bandsaw the piece to shape, and then remove the pattern.

9. Using double-faced tape, stick the hood, cab, passenger seat, and

continued

RED HOT FIRE TRUCK
continued

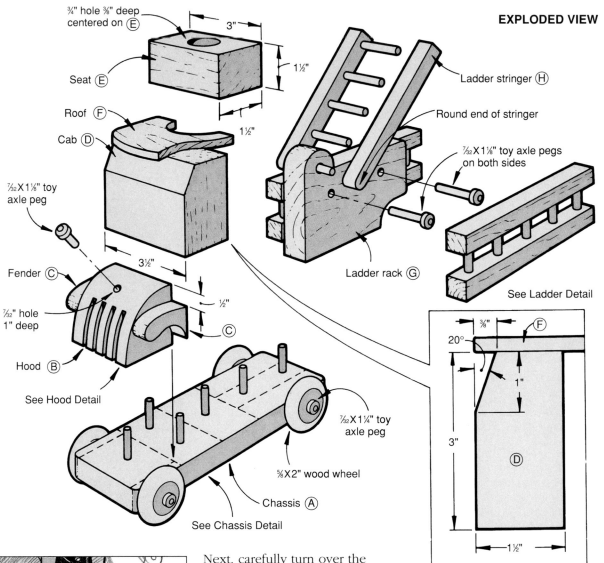

EXPLODED VIEW

¾" hole ⅜" deep centered on Ⓔ

3"

1½"

Seat Ⓔ

1½"

Roof Ⓕ

Cab Ⓓ

Ladder stringer Ⓗ

Round end of stringer

⁷⁄₃₂ X 1⅛" toy axle peg

⁷⁄₃₂ X 1⅛" toy axle pegs on both sides

Fender Ⓒ

⁷⁄₃₂" hole 1" deep

Hood Ⓑ

See Hood Detail

3½"

½"

Ⓒ

Ladder rack Ⓖ

See Ladder Detail

⁷⁄₃₂ X 1¼" toy axle peg

⅝ X 2" wood wheel

Chassis Ⓐ

See Chassis Detail

CAB DETAIL

⅜"

Ⓕ

20°

1"

3"

Ⓓ

1½"

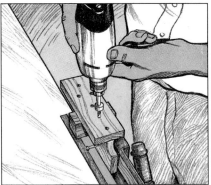

Next, carefully turn over the assembly, and drill through the six ¼" holes in the template and 1⅛" into the fire truck parts (B, D, E, and G) as shown at *left*. Remove the parts from the template, and enlarge the holes you just drilled in the pieces to ⁷⁄₃₂"; the larger holes will make it easier for a child to remove and replace the truck parts on the dowels. Now, check the fit of all parts on the truck's chassis.

Build the ladders and you're nearly finished

1. From ¾" pine, rip and crosscut six ½ X ½ X 5" pieces for the ladder

ladder rack in position on the top face of the chassis template where indicated by the dashed lines on the Chassis drawing.

stringers (H). Next, make a drilling template by sawing a piece of ¼"-thick hardboard to the same length and width. Lay out the centerpoints for the rung holes on the face of the hardboard, using the dimensions on the Ladder detail *opposite, top left*. Now, carefully drill the ¼" holes through the hardboard.

2. Place the hardboard template on top of a ladder stringer, and using your drill press, drill through a template hole and ¼" deep into the stringer. (We set the stop on our

46

LADDER DETAIL

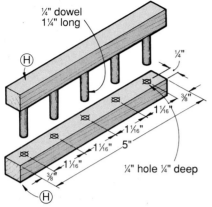

¼" dowel 1¼" long

Ⓗ

¼"

³⁄₈"

1¹⁄₁₆"

1¹⁄₁₆"

1¹⁄₁₆"   5"

1¹⁄₁₆"

³⁄₈"

¼" hole ¼" deep

Ⓗ

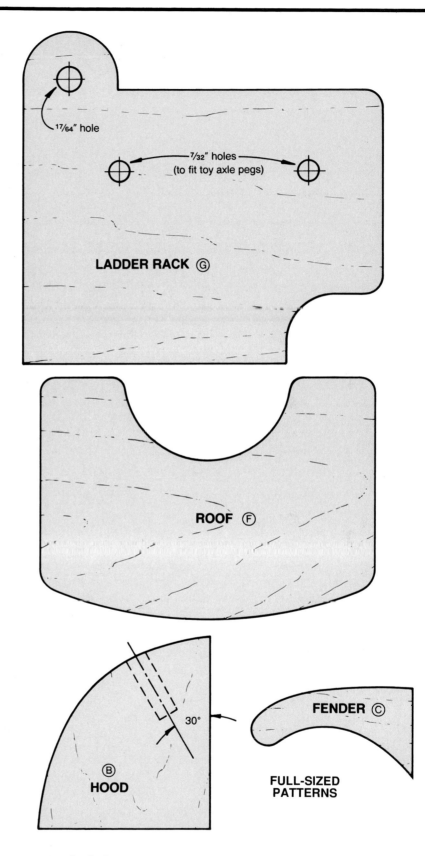

LADDER RACK Ⓖ

¹⁷⁄₆₄" hole

⁷⁄₃₂" holes
(to fit toy axle pegs)

ROOF Ⓕ

30°

Ⓑ
HOOD

FENDER Ⓒ

FULL-SIZED
PATTERNS

drill press to control the depth.) Next, drill all five holes in the stringer. Drill the other five stringers the same way.

3. Cut 15—¼" dowels 1¼" long for the ladder rungs. Glue and assemble two of the ladders.

4. Round one end on the two remaining ladder stringers where shown on the Exploded View drawing. (We shaped the ends with our disc sander.) Glue the rungs in the holes of one stringer, insert the bottom rung through the top hole in the ladder rack, and then finish assembling that ladder.

5. Glue four ⁷⁄₃₂ X 1⅛" toy axle pegs in the holes drilled in the ladder rack (two on each side).

6. Slip a ⅛ X 2" wheel and ¼" flat washer over a ⁷⁄₃₂ X 1⅛" toy axle peg. Apply glue in one of the holes of the chassis, and then insert the assembled axle peg into the hole. Now, repeat this procedure for the other wheels. For the radiator cap, shorten the shaft on an axle peg to ½" long, and glue it in the hole you drilled earlier in the hood.

7. Apply the finish of your choice. (We brushed on two coats of acrylic paint. We painted the axle pegs and ladder holders blue, the body red, and the ladders yellow. The wheels were left natural.)

Project Tool List
Tablesaw
Bandsaw
Disc sander
Drill
Drill Press
  Bits: ⁷⁄₃₂", ¼", ¹⁷⁄₆₄", ¾"
Finishing sander

Note: *We built the project using the tools listed. You may be able to substitute other tools or equipment for listed items you don't* *have. Additional common tools and clamps may be required to complete the project.*

THE LEARNING TRAIN

Harold Rupert, a teacher of educationally handicapped elementary students, combined his professional background along with his love of woodworking to create this inspiring toy. His colorful train won the professional puzzle award in *WOOD*® Magazine's 1991 Build-A-Toy™ competition.

Let's put the engine at the head of the line

1. For the engine chassis (A), rip and crosscut a piece of 1¹⁄₁₆"-thick stock to 2×7". (We used maple.) Copy the train patterns on *page 52* (we photocopied ours), and then cut out the two Engine Chassis patterns. To shape the cowcatcher, adhere the Top View pattern to the top front of the piece and the Side View pattern to the front left side

with rubber cement or spray adhesive. Next, set your tablesaw blade at 45° from perpendicular, and bevel-cut the front end. Without changing the saw blade, angle your miter gauge to 45°, and then as shown *below,* miter-cut both front corners of the chassis to match the pattern lines. Round over all edges. Then, remove the patterns.

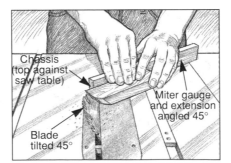

Chassis (top against saw table)

Miter gauge and extension angled 45°

Blade tilted 45°

2. Using dimensions on the Engine Chassis drawing, lay out the centerpoints for the four ⅜" holes on the top, and then drill them ⅜" deep. Next, rip and crosscut a piece of maple stock to ⅜×2×2" for the undercarriage (B). Glue and clamp it to the base where shown on the Engine Chassis drawing *opposite.* Wipe off excess glue with a damp cloth.

3. Mark the locations of the two ⁷⁄₁₆" axle holes and the ⁵⁄₁₆" axle hole on the chassis side. Drill these holes through the chassis. (We backed all parts with scrap to prevent chip-out when drilling holes through them.)

4. To make the engine barrel (C), rip and crosscut a piece of eight- quarter (1¾") pine stock to 1⅞" wide and 12" long. (We initially cut the piece extra long for safety while making the saw cuts.) Next, mark and drill the two ½"-diameter vertical holes through your blank as dimensioned on the Barrel detail on *page 50.* (We used brad-point bits to drill these holes.)

Note: *Designer Harold Rupert suggests making the barrel from hand-rail stock since the two profiles nearly match. He reports that many lumberyards often have short lengths of hand rail left over that you can buy reasonably.*

5. Using scissors, cut out the Engine Barrel (End View) pattern. Next, center and adhere the pattern to the front end of the barrel blank. Now, drill the ⁷⁄₃₂" hole ½" deep into the front of the barrel where indicated on the pattern.

6. To shape the engine barrel, first tilt your tablesaw blade to 30° from perpendicular. Next, as shown *opposite,* bevel-rip the corners of the blank to start rounding the barrel, but take care to stay outside the pattern line. Cut a 4" length from the piece, and then finish rounding it to the pattern line by sanding the piece on your belt sander. Remove the pattern.

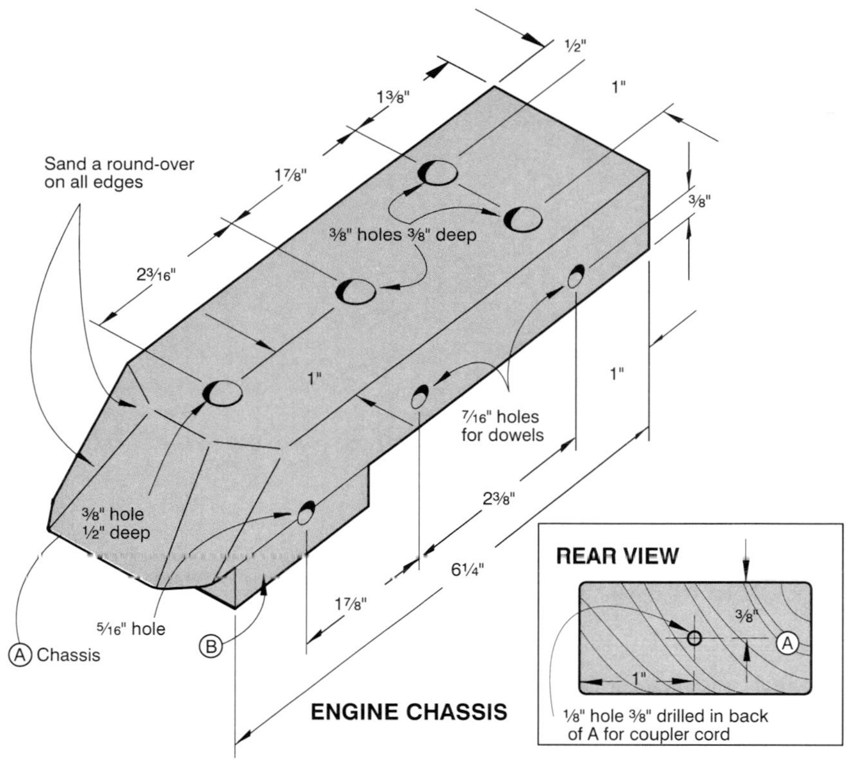

Sand a round-over on all edges
1⁄2"
1"
1 3⁄8"
1 7⁄8"
3⁄8" holes 3⁄8" deep
3⁄8"
2 3⁄16"
1"
1"
7⁄16" holes for dowels
3⁄8" hole 1⁄2" deep
2 3⁄8"
6 1⁄4"
1 7⁄8"
5⁄16" hole
(A) Chassis
(B)
ENGINE CHASSIS
REAR VIEW
3⁄8"
1"
(A)
1⁄8" hole 3⁄8" drilled in back of A for coupler cord

Bill of Materials					
Part	Finished Size			Mat.	Qty.
	T	W	L		
ENGINE					
A chassis	1 1⁄16"	2"	7"	M	1
B under-carriage	3⁄8"	2"	2"	M	1
C barrel	1 3⁄4"	1 3⁄4"	4"	P	1
D cab	2"	2 1⁄8"	2 1⁄2"	P	1
E roof	1⁄2"	2 3⁄4"	2 3⁄4"	M	1
F link	1⁄8"	3⁄4"	3 11⁄16"	W	2
FREIGHT CARS AND LOADS					
G chassis	1 1⁄16"	2"	5"	M	3
H platform	1⁄2"	3"	5 3⁄4"	M	3
I triangles	1 1⁄16"	1 1⁄2"	3"	M	8
J rectangle	1 1⁄16"	2"	4"	M	1
K square	1 1⁄16"	2"	2	M	2
L rectangle	1⁄2"	2 3⁄4"	4 1⁄2"	M	1
M square	3⁄4"	1"	1"	M	2
N square	2"	2"	2"	M	2

Material Key: M–maple; P–pine, W–walnut
Supplies: 1 1⁄4" and 2" wood wheels, smoke-stack, 1⁄2" screw-hole button, 7⁄32" toy axle pegs, 1⁄8" drapery-rod cord, 3⁄8"dowel, 1⁄4" dowel, Velcro fastener, paint, finish.

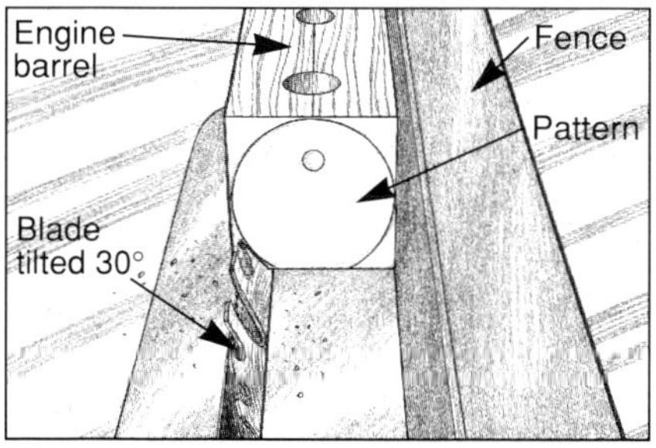

Engine barrel
Fence
Pattern
Blade tilted 30°

7. For the engine's cab (D), rip and crosscut a piece of pine stock to the dimensions listed on the Bill of Materials *above right*. (We used 4X4 pine.) Next, cut the Cab Side View pattern to shape and adhere it to one side of the cab blank. Lay out the centerpoints for the two 1⁄2" holes in the top of the cab blank, and then drill both. Following the pattern outline, bandsaw the cab back, sawing just outside the line. Sand the sawed radius to the line. (We sanded ours on the end of a stationary belt sander.) Remove the pattern and round over all cab edges.

8. To make the cab's roof (E), saw a piece of stock to the dimensions listed on the Bill of Materials. Locate the centerpoints for the two 1⁄2" holes, and drill them through the piece. Round over all roof edges.

9. Rip and crosscut a piece of 3⁄4"-thick scrap walnut to 1" wide and 12" long. Resaw a 1⁄8"-thick strip from the piece. Crosscut this strip in half, and using double-faced tape, stick the two together face-to-face. Next, adhere the Link pattern to one piece, and then drill the 1⁄4" and 7⁄32" holes where marked on the pattern. Now, scrollsaw the two links (F) to shape, cut out the slot, and then separate the two parts. (We used a #5 scrollsaw blade.) Finish-sand both pieces.

We'll make three freight cars

Note: *Although our freight cars carry different loads, we used the same dimensions when constructing them, as indicated on the Car 1 drawing. The Bill of Materials lists the number of parts needed to make three cars. To make a longer train, increase the number of parts and make them at the same time. Car 2 and Car 3 have an identical platform.*

1. For the freight cars chassis (G), rip and crosscut three pieces of 1 1⁄16"-thick maple to the dimensions listed on the Bill of Materials. Next, mark the centerpoints for the 5⁄16"-axle holes on the side of each chassis where shown on the Car 1 Exploded View drawing on *page 51*. Drill these holes through each car chassis. Now, using a 1⁄4"-piloted round-over bit, round over the bottom edges on each car chassis.

2. From 1⁄2"-thick stock, rip and crosscut a platform (H) for each car, using the dimension on the Bill of Materials. Finish-sand the platforms and chassis. Sand a round-over along all platform edges.

3. Center, glue, and clamp a car chassis to the underside of each platform. Next, locate the hole centerpoints for the load-support dowels on each platform top. Use the Car 1 drawing to lay out the Car 1 platform; refer to the Car 3 drawing for details on cars 2 and 3. Drill the holes as dimensioned on both Car 1 and Car 3 drawings. Or, design your own loads and dowel arrangements.

4. Rip and crosscut the freight rectangles, squares, and triangles (I, J, K, L, M, and N) as dimensioned

continued

THE LEARNING TRAIN
continued

EXPLODED VIEW

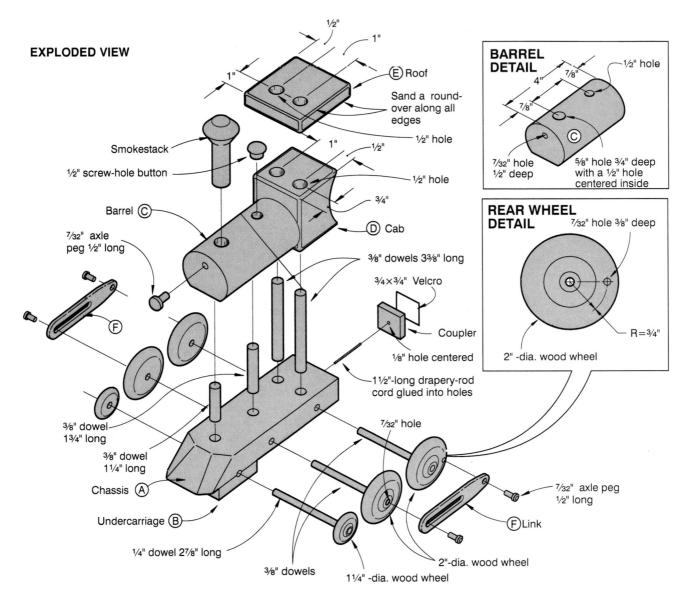

½"

1"

1"

(E) Roof

Sand a round-over along all edges

½" hole

Smokestack

½" screw-hole button

1"

½"

½" hole

¾"

(D) Cab

Barrel (C)

⁷⁄₃₂" axle peg ½" long

⅜" dowels 3⅜" long

¾ × ¾" Velcro

Coupler

⅛" hole centered

1½"-long drapery-rod cord glued into holes

⅜" dowel 1¾" long

⅜" dowel 1¼" long

Chassis (A)

Undercarriage (B)

¼" dowel 2⅞" long

⁷⁄₃₂" hole

⁷⁄₃₂" axle peg ½" long

(F) Link

⅜" dowels

1¼"-dia. wood wheel

2"-dia. wood wheel

(F)

BARREL DETAIL

4"

⁷⁄₈"

½" hole

⁷⁄₈"

(C)

⁷⁄₈"

⁷⁄₃₂" hole ½" deep

⅝" hole ¾" deep with a ½" hole centered inside

REAR WHEEL DETAIL

⁷⁄₃₂" hole ⅜" deep

R = ¾"

2"-dia. wood wheel

---

on the Bill of Materials. Lay out the hole centerpoints, and then drill the ½" holes through the load pieces where indicated. To saw the triangular-load pieces, cut the stock to thickness and width. Angle the miter gauge to 45°, and then cut one end. Adhere the pattern to the end of the piece, and set a stop-block on your rip fence. Now, make the miter cut to complete the first triangle. Cut additional triangles by turning the piece over to make the second miter-cut as shown on *page 52*. Use the pattern to find the hole centerpoint.

5. To make the car couplers, first rip a piece of ¾"-thick maple to ¾" wide and 12" long. Next, re-saw a ³⁄₁₆"-wide strip from the piece, and then crosscut six ¾" squares from the ³⁄₁₆"-thick strip. Drill a ¹⁄₁₆" hole through the center of each square.

Right on schedule: Now finish making up the train

1. Crosscut the ⅜" dowels to the lengths specified for the engine and freight cars. Chamfer one end of each dowel. Paint the engine barrel, cab, cab roof, and the freight. (We used spray enamel paints purchased at a crafts store. You may use any child-safe enamel or acrylic paint.)

2. Finish the unpainted train parts. (We applied one coat of clear sanding sealer to the remaining train parts, the smokestack, wheels, screw-hole button, ⅜" dowels, and the large ends of the axle pegs. After the sealer dried, we sanded the parts lightly with 320-grit sandpaper before applying a coat of clear semigloss polyurethane. After it dried, we rubbed lightly with 0000 steel wool.)

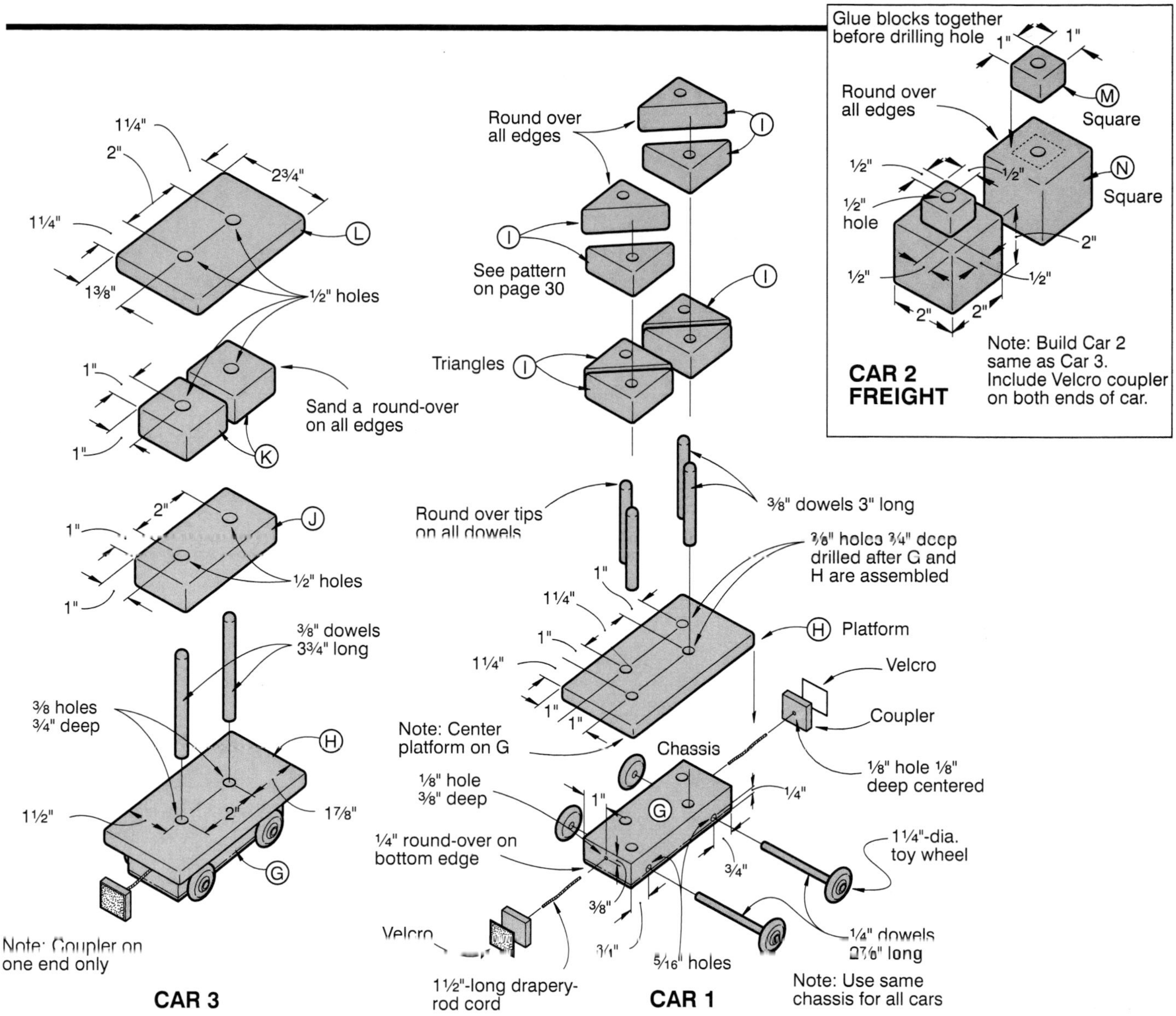

Glue blocks together before drilling hole
1"
1"
Round over all edges
M Square
1/2"
1/2"
1/2" hole
N Square
2"
1/2"
1/2"
2"
2"
CAR 2 FREIGHT
Note: Build Car 2 same as Car 3. Include Velcro coupler on both ends of car.
1 1/4"
2"
2 3/4"
1 1/4"
L
1 3/8"
1/2" holes
1"
1"
Sand a round-over on all edges
K
2"
1"
J
1"
1/2" holes
3/8" dowels 3 3/4" long
3/8 holes 3/4" deep
H
1 1/2"
2"
1 7/8"
G
Note: Coupler on one end only
CAR 3
Round over all edges
I
See pattern on page 30
I
Triangles I
Round over tips on all dowels
3/8" dowels 3" long
3/8" holes 3/4" deep drilled after G and H are assembled
1"
1 1/4"
1"
1 1/4"
H Platform
Velcro
Coupler
1"
1"
Note: Center platform on G
Chassis
1/8" hole 1/8" deep centered
1/8" hole 3/8" deep
1"
G
1/4"
1/4" round-over on bottom edge
1 1/4"-dia. toy wheel
3/4"
3/8"
Velcro
3/4"
5/16" holes
1/4" dowels 2 7/8" long
1 1/2"-long drapery-rod cord
CAR 1
Note: Use same chassis for all cars

3. Glue the dowels, smokestack, screw-hole button, and axle peg in the appropriate holes.

4. From 3/8" dowel, crosscut one 3¼" length and one 3⅛" length. Crosscut one 2⅞" length of ¼" dowel. Glue a 2" wood wheel to one end of the 3¼"-long dowel, and extend the dowel 1/16" beyond the wheel face. Insert the dowel axle into the center hole in the engine chassis and glue a 2" wheel onto the end of the dowel so it also extends 1/16" beyond the wheel face on that side, too. Now, drill a 7/32" hole 3/8" deep into the center of both ends of that axle dowel.

5. Insert the shafts of 7/32" axle pegs through the slots of the wheel links, and then glue the wooden pegs in the holes in the ends of the centerwheel axle.

6. Referring to the Rear Wheel detail drawing *opposite*, mark and drill a 7/32" hole where shown on the outside face of two 2" wooden wheels. Drill these holes 3/8" deep. Next, glue and assemble these rear wheels and the 3⅛"-long axle in the rear-axle hole of the engine chassis as shown on the Exploded View drawing. Before this glue sets, insert a ½"-long axle peg through the hole in the end of each link, and glue it into the rear wheel hole. Now, twist these two rear wheels on the axle to synchronize the pegs so they align and the wheel links work together smoothly.

7. Next, assemble and glue the 1¼"-diameter wheels and ¼" dowel for the engine's front wheels. Crosscut six 2⅞" lengths of ¼" dowel for the freight-car axles. Assemble and glue these wheels and axles.

8. Mark the centerpoint for holes in the rear of the engine chassis, at both ends of cars 1 and 2, and at one end of Car 3. Drill ⅛" holes 3/8" deep at each mark. To complete the couplings, cut six 1½" lengths of heavy cord. (We used drapery-rod cord.) Glue one of the squares to the end of each piece of cord. (We used cyanoacrylate glue.) Glue the

continued

THE LEARNING TRAIN
continued

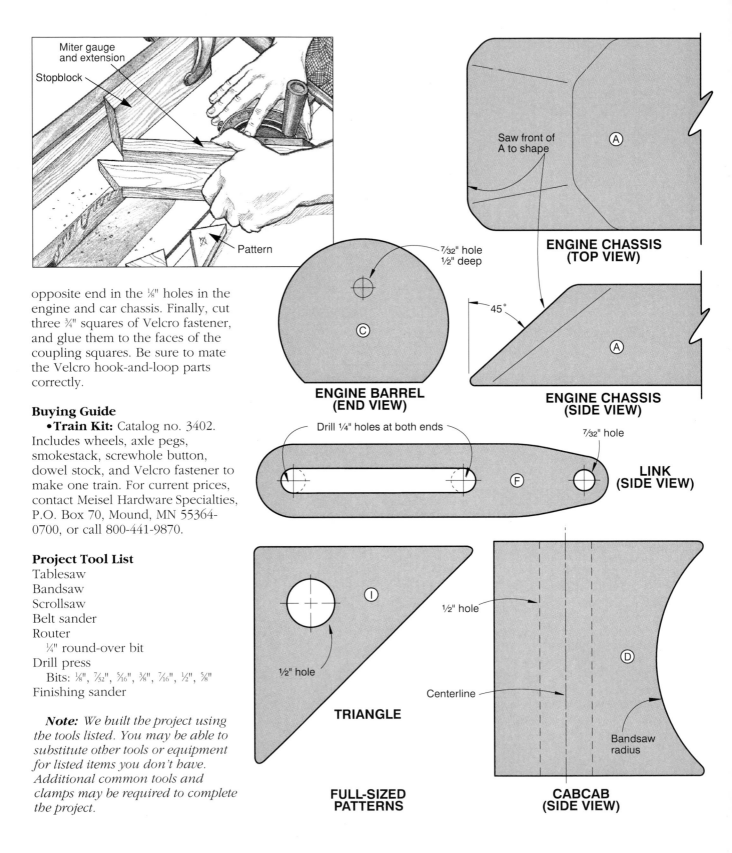

ENGINE CHASSIS (TOP VIEW)

Miter gauge and extension

Stopblock

Pattern

Saw front of A to shape

(A)

45°

(A)

ENGINE CHASSIS (SIDE VIEW)

7/32" hole 1/2" deep

(C)

ENGINE BARREL (END VIEW)

Drill 1/4" holes at both ends

7/32" hole

(F)

LINK (SIDE VIEW)

(I)

1/2" hole

1/2" hole

TRIANGLE

1/2" hole

Centerline

(D)

Bandsaw radius

CABCAB (SIDE VIEW)

FULL-SIZED PATTERNS

opposite end in the ⅛" holes in the engine and car chassis. Finally, cut three ¾" squares of Velcro fastener, and glue them to the faces of the coupling squares. Be sure to mate the Velcro hook-and-loop parts correctly.

Buying Guide
•**Train Kit:** Catalog no. 3402. Includes wheels, axle pegs, smokestack, screwhole button, dowel stock, and Velcro fastener to make one train. For current prices, contact Meisel Hardware Specialties, P.O. Box 70, Mound, MN 55364-0700, or call 800-441-9870.

Project Tool List
Tablesaw
Bandsaw
Scrollsaw
Belt sander
Router
  ¼" round-over bit
Drill press
  Bits: ⅛", 7/32", 5/16", ⅜", 7/16", ½", ⅝"
Finishing sander

Note: We built the project using the tools listed. You may be able to substitute other tools or equipment for listed items you don't have. Additional common tools and clamps may be required to complete the project.

THE U.S.S. WOOD FUNTIME FLEET

Fashion a jig with handscrew clamps and scrap wood drilled with a 1" hole. Use it to secure the 1" dowels while you bore out the centers for smokestacks with a flat-bottomed bit.

Kids love playing with floating toys in the bathtub. They'll love you, too, when you present them with either of these two terrific toy boats. If you're feeling ambitious, give the battleship a try. Or if you want to turn something out in a hurry, take on the tug.

1. Begin by transferring the hull patterns on *page 55* to ½" graph paper. (Be sure to transfer the holes as well as the outline of the hulls.) Then, using carbon paper, transfer the hull shapes and hole locations to your pine stock (A, B, C). Cut the hull pieces to shape with a band saw or portable jigsaw.

2. Drill eight holes in hull A to accommodate the ballast nuts. Clamp A, B, and C together and drill the holes for the hull pins (D). Cut the hull pins to length. Put the ballast nuts in place, then epoxy and clamp the hull pieces (A, B, C, D) together. (The hull pins will protrude ½" above the surface of C for later mounting of the gun turrets.) Sand all surfaces smooth after the epoxy has cured.

3. Transfer the full-sized patterns on *page 55* to tracing paper, then

use carbon paper to transfer them to pine stock. Cut the superstructure (E), the bridge (F), the launch (G, H), the turret (I), and the launch stack (J) to shape. Drill the portholes in E and F, and the gun barrel holes in I where depicted on the Exploded View drawing. (We clamped the pieces in a hand screw to hold them steady while drilling.) Now, bore a ½" hole in the bottom of the turret for later mounting onto part D. Glue E in place on the hull and when the glue dries, mark and drill all the holes in both E and F as the patterns indicate.

4. Epoxy launch parts G and H together, position them on the hull, and drill the hole for J through the launch and into the hull. Epoxy the launches to the hull.

5. Cut the smokestacks (K) to length. Clamp a piece of scrap wood to your drill press table and bore a 1" hole 1" deep in it. Without moving the jig, insert K into the hole and clamp it to prevent it from turning with the bit, switch to a ¾" bit and bore a hole 1¾" deep in the end of each K as shown in the photo *top right.*

To make the crow's nest (L), insert a 1"-diameter dowel that's 1½"

long in the jig and bore a ¾" hole ⁵⁄₁₆" deep. Without moving the dowel or jig, switch to a ½" bit and bore a hole through the center of the ¾" hole all the way through the remaining stock. Hand-cut the top ⅝" off the dowel.

6. Cut the bridge supports (M), barrels (N), mast (O), air ducts (P), bollards (Q), crane shaft (R), crane boom (S), yardarms (T), and mast (U) to length.

7. Epoxy the barrels (N) in the turrets (I). Apply paraffin to each hull pin D and mount the turrets. (This lets the turrets swivel and allows you to "fire" port or starboard without having to change course.) Using a ½" drilling jig similar to the 1" jig just used, drill holes in O and P. Cut the drilled ends of P at 45°.

8. To build the jig shown *above,* drill the first hole the same size as the dowel being drilled, all the way through a piece of scrap. Drill the second hole perpendicular to the first, so it intersects the first hole in the exact center. Now, drill the perpendicular holes in the smokestack (K), mast (O), the bollards (Q), the crane shaft (R), boom (S), and yardarms (T). (You will need to tilt the *continued*

THE U.S.S. WOOD FUNTIME FLEET

continued

Bill of Materials

Part	Finished Size* T	W	L	Mat.	Qty.
A	¾"	4"	12½"	P	1
B	½"	4"	14"	P	1
C	¾"	4"	14"	P	1
D	½" dia.2⅛"			D	2
E	½"	4"	4¾"	P	1
F	½"	1⅝"	3"	P	1
G	½"	¾"	2½"	P	2
H	3/16"	¾"	¾"	P	2
I	½"	1½"	1½"	P	2
J	¼" dia.1⅞"			D	2
K	1" dia. 3½"			D	2
L*	1" dia.⅝"			D	1
M	¼" dia.2⅝"			D	2
N	¼" dia.1½"			D	4
O	½" dia.3"			D	1
P	½" dia.1¾"			D	2
Q	½" dia.1"			D	2
R	½" dia.2¾"			D	1
S	¼" dia.2¼"			D	1
T	¼" dia.1¾"			D	2
U	¼" dia.2"			D	1

*Cut to final size during construction. Please read instructions before cutting.

Material Key: P–pine, D–dowel.
Supplies: epoxy or resorcinol (waterproof glues), oil-based enamel paints (rust, gray, black), 8—5/16" nuts

drill press when drilling R.) Glue and install part S into R and into K and O. Chamfer the tops of Q and glue them into the hull. Assemble and install the mast pieces (L, O, T, U).

9. Paint all parts as shown in the photo on *page 53*. (We wiped off the top deck right after painting to imitate the teak decks on real battleships.) When the paint has dried, glue the bridge supports (M) in place and glue the bridge (F) to the supports, ½" above the superstructure. Install the smokestacks (K), air vents (P), and crane assembly (S, R).

Project Tool List

Bandsaw, scrollsaw, or portable jigsaw
Drill
Drill press
Bits: 1/16", ¼", ½", ⅝", ¾", 1"
Finishing sander

EXPLODED VIEW

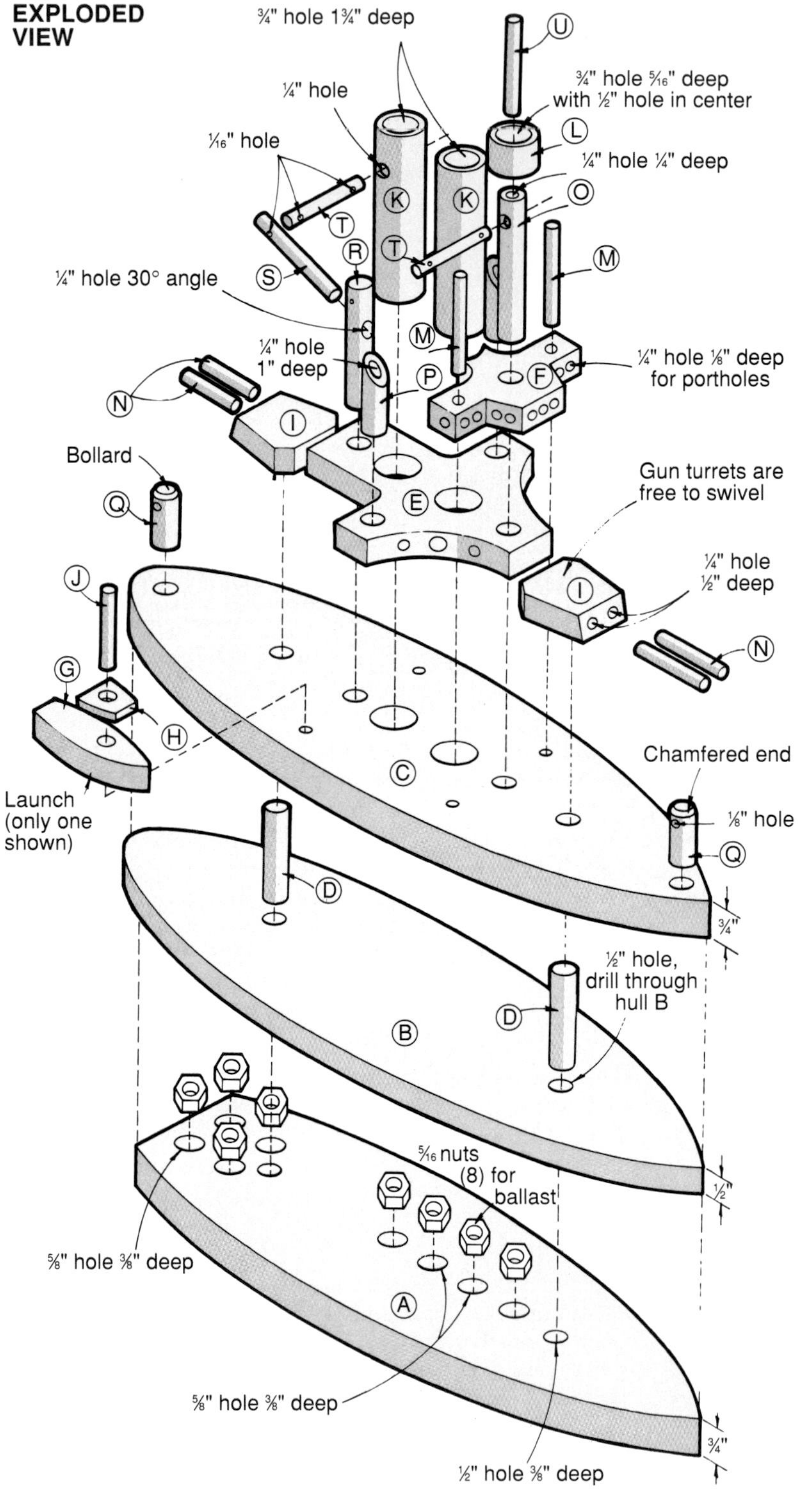

¾" hole 1¾" deep
¼" hole
¾" hole 5/16" deep with ½" hole in center
1/16" hole
¼" hole ¼" deep
¼" hole 30° angle
¼" hole 1" deep
¼" hole ⅛" deep for portholes
Bollard
Gun turrets are free to swivel
¼" hole ½" deep
Chamfered end
⅛" hole
Launch (only one shown)
¾"
½" hole, drill through hull B
5/16 nuts (8) for ballast
½"
⅝" hole ⅜" deep
⅝" hole ⅜" deep
½" hole ⅜" deep
¾"
U
L
O
K
K
T
T
R
S
M
M
N
I
P
F
Q
E
J
I
N
G
H
C
Q
D
D
B
A

__Note:__ We built the project using the tools listed. You may be able to substitute other tools or equipment for listed items you don't have. Additional common tools and clamps may be required to complete the project.

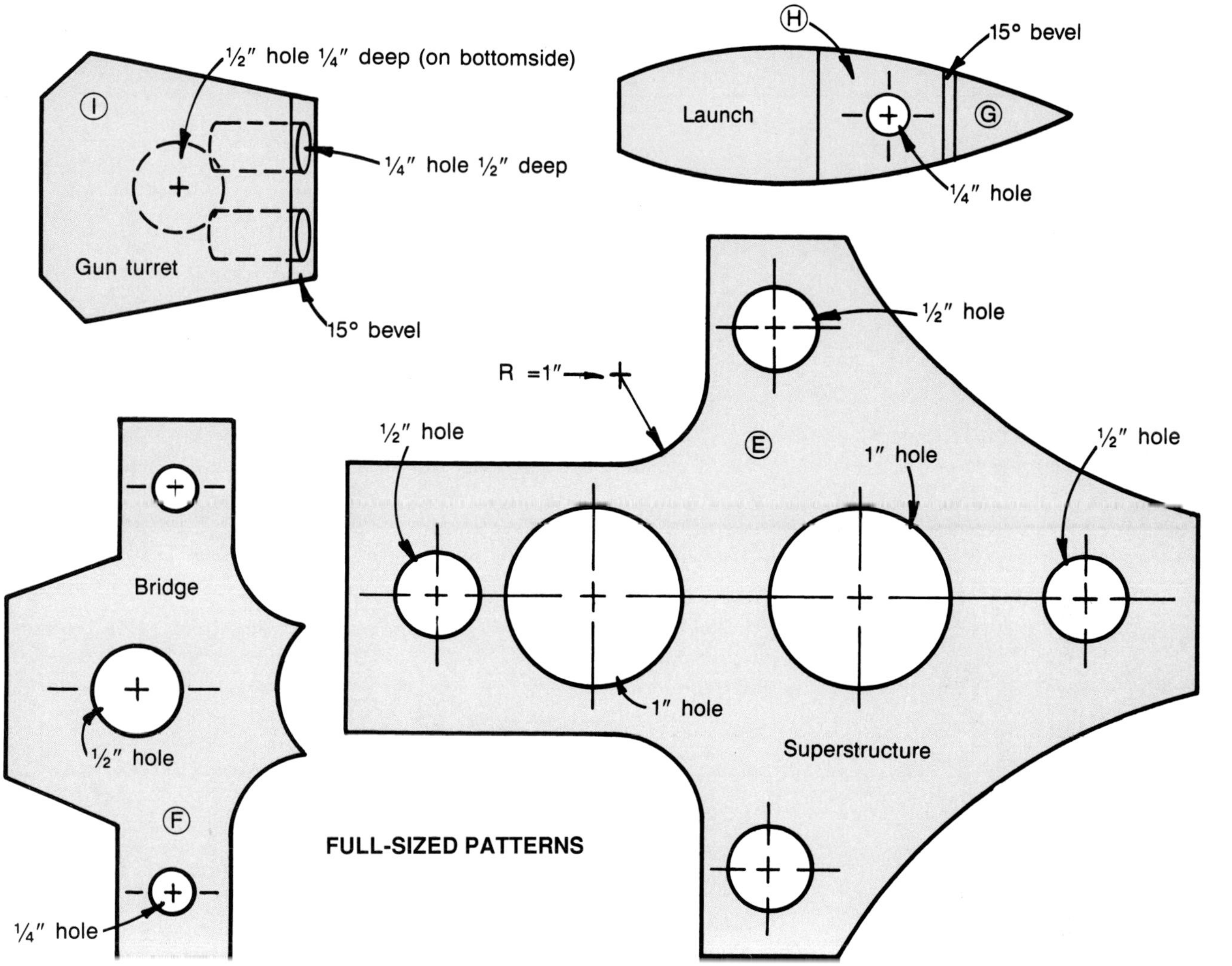
½" hole ¼" deep (on bottomside)
Ⓘ
¼" hole ½" deep
Gun turret
15° bevel
Ⓗ
15° bevel
Launch
Ⓖ
¼" hole
½" hole
R =1"
½" hole
Ⓔ
1" hole
½" hole
Bridge
1" hole
½" hole
Superstructure
Ⓕ
¼" hole

FULL-SIZED PATTERNS

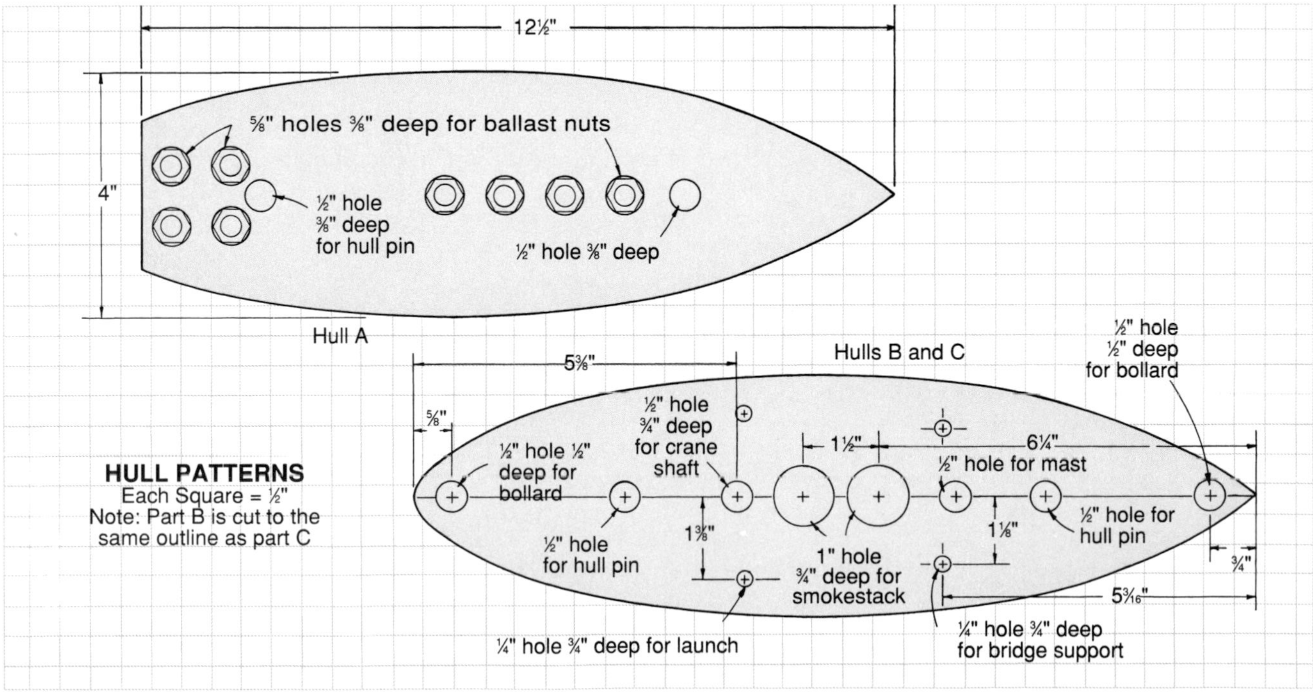
12½"
4"
⅝" holes ⅜" deep for ballast nuts
½" hole
⅜" deep
for hull pin
½" hole ⅜" deep
Hull A
5⅜"
Hulls B and C
½" hole
½" deep
for bollard
⅝"
½" hole
¾" deep
for crane
shaft
½" hole ½"
deep for
bollard
1½"
6¼"
½" hole for mast
½" hole
for hull pin
1⅜"
1" hole
¾" deep for
smokestack
1⅛"
½" hole for
hull pin
¾"
5³⁄₁₆"
¼" hole ¾" deep for launch
¼" hole ¾" deep
for bridge support

HULL PATTERNS
Each Square = ½"
Note: Part B is cut to the same outline as part C

WHIRLYBIRD ON A STRING

Action toys have always held a fascination for youngsters, and this project continues that tradition in fine style. As the child pulls the toy forward, a drive wheel at the bottom of the rotor shaft spins the main rotor. That special someone will love you even more when you surprise him or her with this great little 6½x9½" gift.

Let's start with the body

1. Rip and crosscut a 1½"-thick pine block to 3½x9½" for the whirlybird body (A). (We cut ours from a scrap 2x4.) Cut a second 1½"-thick block to 3½x4" for the angled-support block shown *opposite.*

2. Lay carbon paper and the body's Side View pattern (see *page 59*) on the larger block, align it, and trace the body pattern, including the hole center-points. Using the dimensions on the Front View drawing (also *page 59*), mark the centerpoint of the ¼" hole for the pull cord. Measure and mark the dowel hole centerpoints and the main rotor shaft hole centerpoint on the whirlybird bottom, referring to the Body Block drawing *opposite, top right.*

3. Referring to the Making and Using the Angled-Support Block drawing *opposite,* lay out the location of the block's angled notch. To do this, strike a horizontal line ⅞" down from the top face of the support. Measure in 1¼" along the line, and mark a point. Mark a second point near the top lefthand corner of the block where shown. Hold a square to the points, with the inside corner of the square directly over the lower point. Now, strike a line along the square's inside edge. Using a band saw, cut the ⅞"-deep notch.

4. Rest the body block (A) upside down in the angled support on a drill press table. Using a ¼" bit, drill the four ½"-deep holes in the body. Remove the support, and drill a ½"-deep hole for the rear rotor, and a ¼x1"-deep hole for the pull-cord pin. Change to a ⁷⁄₁₆" bit, and drill the vertical hole through the whirlybird body for the main rotor shaft. Switch to a 1½" hole saw or bit, and cut out the window. Back the body with scrap wood to prevent chip-out.

5. Cut the body to shape, following the pattern line. Sand off any saw marks as well as splinters around the holes.

And now for the landing skids

1. Rip and crosscut two ¾x1x6½" pine blocks for the skids (B).

2. Referring to the Landing Skid drawing *opposite,* lay out the hole center points for both skids. You'll need ⁷⁄₃₂" holes ½" deep for the wheel axles, angled ¼" holes ½" deep for the dowels connecting the skids to the body, and, on the inside left skid only, a centered ⁷⁄₃₂" hole ½" deep for the drive-wheel axle. Drill the angled holes, using the angled support block. Sand the skids smooth.

3. Paint the 1½"-diameter wheels (see the Buying Guide for our source of toy parts). While the paint is drying, cut four ¼" dowels to 2" long. Apply glue to the dowel ends, and insert them into the body block. Now, add the landing skids, checking that the bottoms are parallel.

4. Thread the axle pegs through the five skid wheels, apply glue to their tips, and insert in the skids' remaining holes. (Be careful not to pinch the wheels between the pegs and skids; this would prevent the wheels from turning freely.)

Here's how to make and install the rotors and pull cord

1. Using the full-size half patterns on *page 59*, trace the tail and main rotors (C, D)—including the dowel hole centerpoints—onto ½" stock, and cut them to shape on a band-saw. Sand the two rotors smooth. (We drum-sanded the curved surfaces and hand-sanded the rest.)

Drill a ¼" hole in the tail rotor and a ⅜" hole in the main rotor.

2. Paint the rotors and the 2"-diameter main rotor-drive wheel. And while these dry, cut the ⅜" main rotor shaft dowel to 5 inches long.

3. For a smooth-rotating main rotor, apply paraffin to the sections of the rotor shaft dowel that will be in contact with the whirlybird body. Apply glue to one end of the main rotor shaft, and insert it into the hole in the large rotor. Fit the shaft through the vertical hole in the body, add glue to the lower end, and slip on the 2"-diameter wheel.

4. Insert the tail rotor's axle through the ¼" hole in the tail rotor, and glue and insert its tip into the appropriate hole in the whirlybird body.

5. Clamp a 1" wooden ball in a wood handscrew, and drill a ¼" hole ½" deep in it. (We did this on a drill press.) Insert one end of the pull cord in the ball's hole, and secure it with an axle peg glued in place. Secure the cord's other end in the body the same way.

Buying Guide
• **Whirlybird kit.** Catalog no. 3401. Includes enough wooden wheels, balls, axle pegs, dowel stock, and cord to make four toys. For current prices, contact Meisel Hardware Specialties, P.O. Box 70, Mound, MN 55364-0700, or call 800-441-9870.

continued

BODY BLOCK

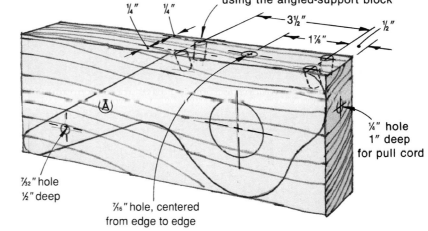

LANDING SKID

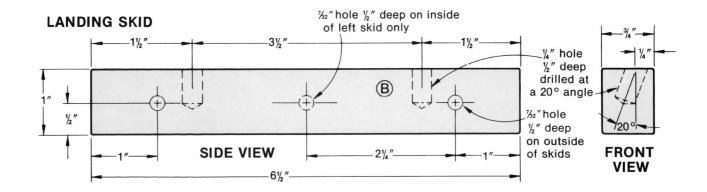

WHIRLYBIRD ON A STRING

continued

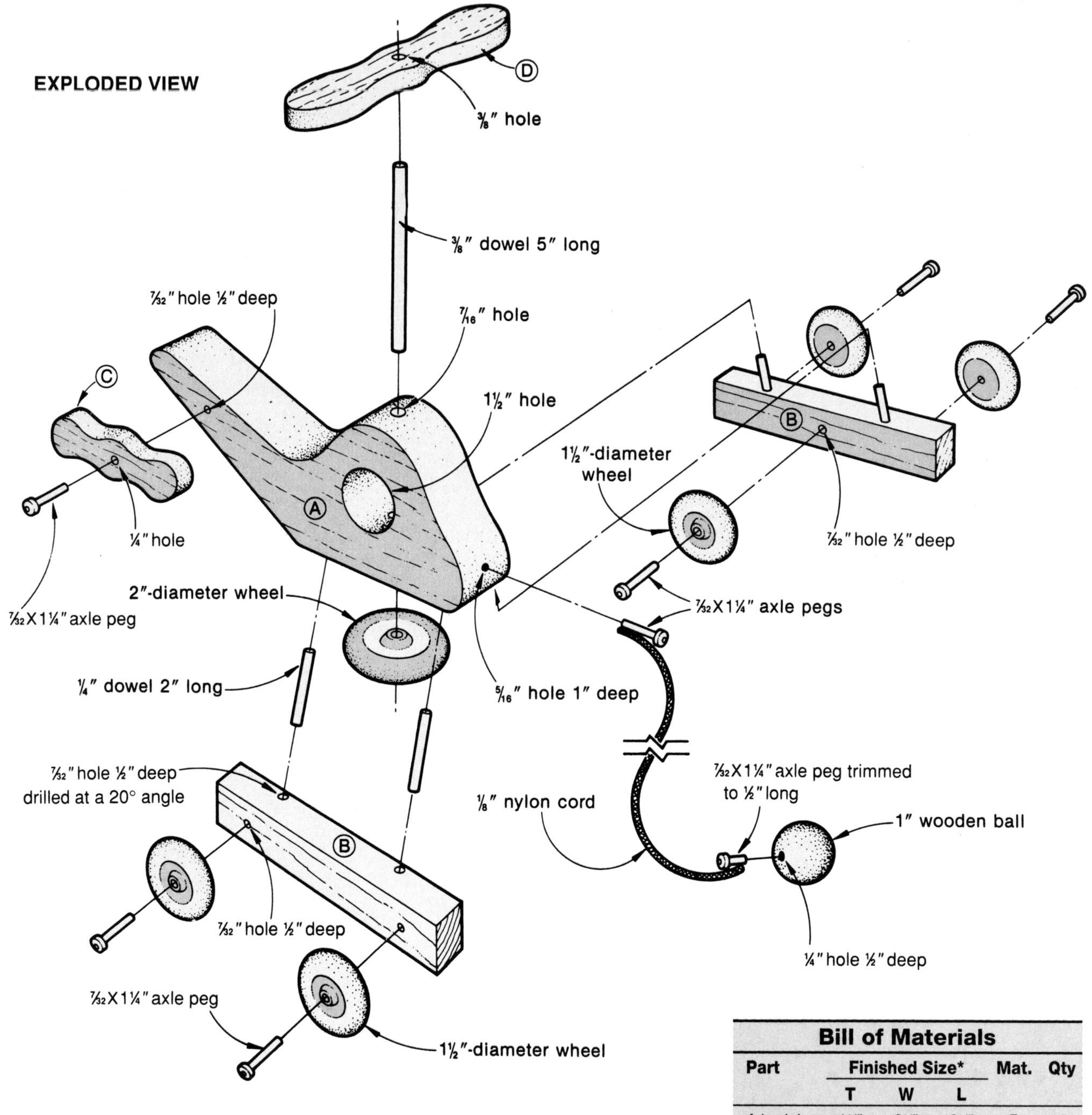
EXPLODED VIEW
D
3/8" hole
3/8" dowel 5" long
7/32" hole 1/2" deep
7/16" hole
C
1 1/2" hole
1 1/2"-diameter wheel
B
7/32" hole 1/2" deep
A
1/4" hole
7/32X1 1/4" axle peg
2"-diameter wheel
7/32X1 1/4" axle pegs
1/4" dowel 2" long
5/16" hole 1" deep
7/32" hole 1/2" deep drilled at a 20° angle
1/8" nylon cord
7/32X1 1/4" axle peg trimmed to 1/2" long
1" wooden ball
B
7/32" hole 1/2" deep
1/4" hole 1/2" deep
7/32X1 1/4" axle peg
1 1/2"-diameter wheel

Project Tool List
Tablesaw
Bandsaw
Drill press
- Sanding drum
- 1 1/2", holesaw
- Bits: 1/4", 5/16", 3/8", 7/16"

Finishing sander

Note: *We built the project using the tools listed. You may be able to substitute other tools or equipment for listed items you don't have. Additional common tools and clamps may be required to complete the project.*

Bill of Materials

Part	Finished Size* T	W	L	Mat.	Qty
A body*	1 1/2"	3 1/2"	9 1/2"	P	1
B skids	3/4"	1"	6 1/2"	P	2
C tail rotor	1/2"	1 1/8"	3 3/4"	P	1
D main rotor	1/2"	1 11/16"	7"	P	1

* Cut part larger initially, and then trim to finished size. Please read the instructions before cutting.

Material Key: P–pine
Supplies: carbon paper, 1/8X16 1/2" nylon cord, nontoxic paint or dyes, 1/4" and 3/8" dowel stock

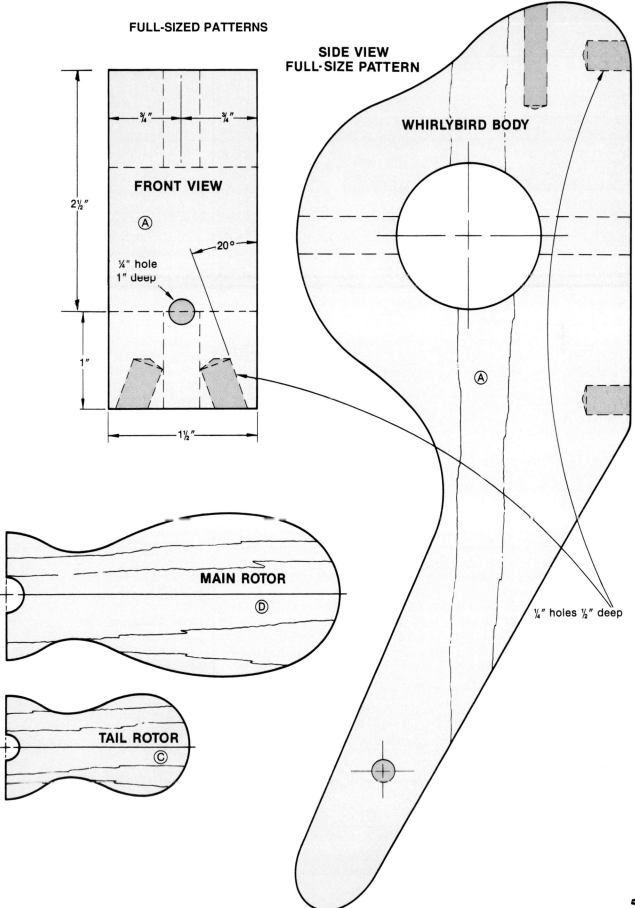

FULL-SIZED PATTERNS

SIDE VIEW
FULL-SIZE PATTERN

WHIRLYBIRD BODY

FRONT VIEW

Ⓐ

¾″   ¾″

2½″

20°

¼″ hole
1″ deep

1″

1½″

¼″ holes ½″ deep

MAIN ROTOR

Ⓓ

TAIL ROTOR

Ⓒ

Ⓐ

59

LI'L SOD-BUSTER TOY TRACTOR

Spring has arrived and it's time to get the crops in the field. Our heavy-duty tractor stands at the ready, waiting for a child's hand to guide it over the sandbox landscapes and rugged terrains of America's backyards. We used walnut wheels to contrast with the maple body, cab, and fenders, and added numerous realistic details. With our full-sized patterns you can create an exact replica of what you see pictured in the farm scene *above.*

Start with the tractor body and fenders

1. Rip and crosscut a piece of 1½"-thick hardwood to 3½x9". (We used maple for all tractor parts except the wheels.) Using carbon paper, transfer the full-sized Body pattern (A) on *page 63*, including the dotted lines, to the wood block.

2. Cut the tractor body to shape on a bandsaw or scrollsaw. (We cut outside the line; then sanded to the line.)

3. Using the Exploded View drawing and Tractor Hitch detail *opposite,* mark the centerpoints for the hitch, exhaust pipe, and air cleaner holes. Drill the holes.

4. Draw a vertical line in the center of the front of the tractor body for the grille. Then, mark four additional lines on both sides, spacing each ⅛" apart. Now, make a 10° wedge-shaped block from scrap the same thickness and length as the body piece. Fit it under the tractor body and tape the two together as shown *below.* (We set the wedge ¹⁄₁₆" back from the front of the body to serve as a cutting depth gauge.) Adjust the

band saw guide to clear the workpiece and align the saw blade with a vertical grille line. Pull the work into the blade and cut a ¹⁄₁₆"-deep saw kerf. Saw all nine grille kerfs this way. Remove the wedge.

5. Turn the tractor body upside down and mark a centerline running 1½" from the front. Mark a crosswise reference line ⅝" back from the front. (You'll use them to align the axle.)

6. Round-over the edges of the tractor body where shown on the Exploded View drawing, *opposite.* (We used a table-mounted router fitted with a ¼" round-over bit for this.)

7. To form the fenders (B), rip and crosscut two 1½"-thick maple blocks to 2¼ x3¾". Using carbon paper, transfer the full-sized Fender pattern to each block. Now cut the fenders to shape and sand smooth.

8. Mark the location of the headlights where shown on the Exploded View drawing. Then, drill the two holes in each fender. (See the drawing, *below,* for how we clamped the fenders and used a tape depth gauge on the drill bit for drilling the holes for the headlights.) Glue a ⅜" button in each headlight hole.

Next, make the cab
Note: You will need some ¼"-thick stock for the tractor cab sides and roof. You can resaw or plane thicker stock to the correct thickness or special order it. See the Buying Guide on page 62 for our source.

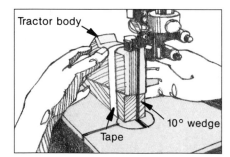

Tractor body

Tape 10° wedge

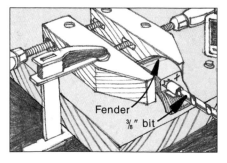

Fender

⅜" bit

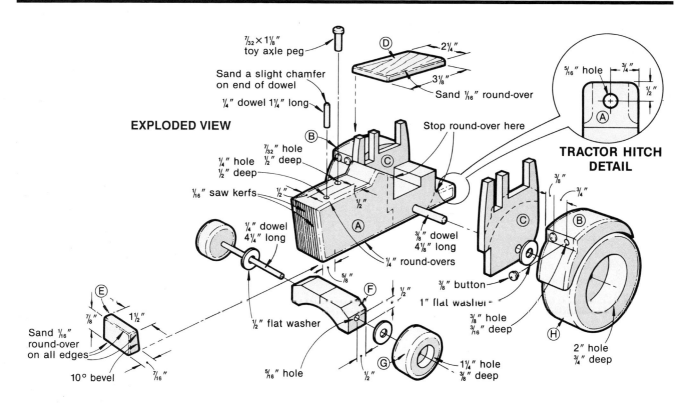

EXPLODED VIEW

$\frac{7}{32} \times 1\frac{1}{8}$" toy axle peg

Sand a slight chamfer on end of dowel

$\frac{1}{4}$" dowel $1\frac{1}{4}$" long

$\frac{7}{32}$" hole $\frac{1}{2}$" deep

$\frac{1}{4}$" hole $\frac{1}{2}$" deep

$\frac{1}{16}$" saw kerfs

$\frac{1}{4}$" dowel $4\frac{1}{4}$" long

Sand $\frac{1}{16}$" round-over on all edges

10° bevel

$\frac{7}{8}$" $1\frac{1}{2}$" $\frac{7}{16}$"

Stop round-over here

Sand $\frac{1}{16}$" round-over

$2\frac{1}{4}$" $3\frac{1}{8}$"

$\frac{1}{4}$" round-overs

$\frac{3}{8}$" dowel $4\frac{1}{8}$" long

$\frac{1}{2}$" $\frac{1}{2}$" $\frac{1}{2}$"

$\frac{1}{2}$" flat washer

$\frac{5}{16}$" hole

$\frac{5}{8}$" $\frac{1}{2}$"

$\frac{3}{8}$" button

1" flat washer

$\frac{3}{8}$" hole $\frac{3}{16}$" deep

$1\frac{1}{4}$" hole $\frac{3}{8}$" deep

2" hole $\frac{3}{4}$" deep

$\frac{3}{8}$" $\frac{3}{4}$" $\frac{3}{8}$" $\frac{3}{4}$"

TRACTOR HITCH DETAIL

$\frac{5}{16}$" hole $\frac{3}{4}$" $\frac{1}{2}$"

1. To make the cab walls (C), rip and crosscut two pieces of $\frac{1}{4}$"-thick maple to $3\frac{1}{4} \times 4\frac{1}{8}$". Using carbon paper, transfer the full-sized cab wall pattern to both pieces and mark the center point for the rear axle hole on one. Cut both cab wall pieces to shape on a bandsaw or scrollsaw. Sand them smooth and sand a slight round-over on all outside edges.

2. Glue and clamp the cab walls to the tractor body. (We aligned the walls with the dotted cab outlines we had drawn on the body and made certain they were even on top to accept the roof.) After the glue dries, remove the clamps and drill the $\frac{7}{16}$" axle hole through the body and cab assembly on a drill press.

3. Again, using $\frac{1}{4}$"-thick maple stock, cut the cab roof (D) to the size listed in the Bill of Materials. Sand a round-over along the top edges. Center and glue it to the top of the cab walls.

Make the tractor weight and axle support

1. To shape the front weight (E), start with a piece of maple about $1\frac{1}{2} \times 1\frac{1}{2} \times 12$". (For safety, we chose to work with a 12"-long piece.) Set the table saw fence $\frac{7}{16}$" from the

blade and the blade 1" above the table. Tilt the blade 10° from vertical toward the fence and make the first rip pass. (Follow these cutting instructions closely because you'll cut another part from this 12"-long piece in Step 2.) Stop the saw, set the saw blade to 0°, lower it to $\frac{1}{2}$", and set the fence $\frac{7}{8}$" from the blade. Turn the piece a quarter-turn clockwise so you can rip the narrow end of the wedge. Rip the piece; then, crosscut a section of the cutaway strip to $1\frac{1}{2}$". Sand a round-over on all edges of the weight and glue it to the front of the tractor body.

2. To shape the front axle support (F), start with the 12" maple piece used in Step 1. Rip the piece to 1" square; then, crosscut it to 3". Transfer the full-sized pattern shown on *page 63* to the piece. Using the dimensions on the Exploded View drawing *above*, mark the center-point for the $\frac{5}{16}$" axle hole. Clamp the piece vertically with a hand-screw clamp on the drill press and bore a hole through the block. Next, make a crosswise reference mark at the center along the top and one side of the axle support. Then, cut the part to final shape on the band saw. Align the line on the

axle support with the line scribed on the underside of the body. Glue and clamp it to the body.

Shaping the wheels

1. Rip and crosscut two pieces of $\frac{3}{4}$" stock to $2\frac{1}{2}$" square for the front wheels. (We used walnut for all four wheels.) Draw diagonals to find the center

continued

Bill of Materials				
Part	**Finished Size***		**Mat.**	**Qty.**
	T	**W**	**L**		
A* body	$1\frac{1}{2}$"	$3\frac{1}{4}$"	$8\frac{1}{2}$"	M	1
B* fenders	$1\frac{1}{2}$"	$2\frac{1}{16}$"	$3\frac{11}{16}$"	M	2
C* cab wall	$\frac{1}{4}$"	$3\frac{3}{16}$"	$4\frac{1}{8}$"	M	2
D roof	$\frac{1}{4}$"	$2\frac{1}{4}$"	$3\frac{1}{8}$"	M	1
E* weight	$\frac{7}{8}$"	$\frac{7}{16}$"	$1\frac{1}{2}$"	M	1
F axle	1"	1"	3"	M	1
G* wheels	$\frac{3}{4}$"	$2\frac{1}{4}$" dia.		W	2
H* wheels	$\frac{1}{2}$"	$3\frac{3}{4}$" dia.		W	2

* Cut parts larger initially, and then trim to finished size. Please read the instructions before cutting.

Material Key: M–maple W–walnut
Supplies: 4—$\frac{3}{8}$" maple buttons, 1—$\frac{7}{32} \times 1\frac{1}{8}$" toy axle peg, $\frac{1}{4}$" dowel, $\frac{3}{8}$" dowel, 2—1" flat washers, 2—$\frac{1}{2}$" flat washers, 1—$\frac{3}{8} \times 4$" machine bolt with washers and nut, 1—$\frac{1}{4} \times 3$" machine bolt with washers and nut, polyurethane.

LI'L SOD-BUSTER TOY TRACTOR
continued

of each blank. Next, chuck a 1¼" Forstner or spade bit in the drill press. Back the blank with scrap, center the marked center point under the bit, and clamp the blank to the table. Bore a hole ⅜" deep. Now chuck a 2¼" circle cutter to the drill press and cut out the wheel. (Our circle cutter automatically drilled the ¼" axle hole.) Repeat the process to make the other front wheel.

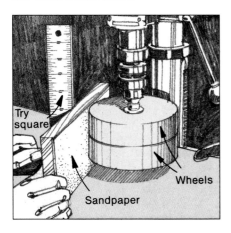

Note: *If you don't have a circle cutter, you can cut the wheels to shape on a band saw. To do so, first draw a 2¼"-diameter circle (1⅛" radius). Then make your cut slightly outside the line. Carefully sand to the line, using the technique described in Step 3.*

2. To form the rear wheels (H), rip and crosscut two pieces of 1½"-thick walnut to 4" square. Follow the procedures outlined in Step 1, using a 2" Forstner bit, a circle cutter, and a ⅜" drill bit (to enlarge the center holes).

3. To true up the rear wheels, thread them to a ⅜ x 4" machine bolt. Chuck this assembly into your drill press and sand as shown *above*. (We adhered half-sheets of

80- and 150-grit sandpaper to particleboard with spray adhesive. To sand, we held it 90° to the table with a try square.) Assemble the front wheels the same way with a ¼ x 3" machine bolt and sand true.

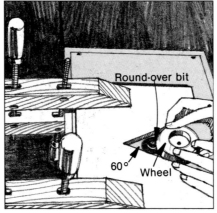

4. Make the V-shaped jig shown *above* to safely round-over the edges of the rear wheels. (We first cut a 60° V in a 1-foot-square scrap of particleboard. Next, we positioned the jig so the wheel contacted the router bit; then, we clamped the jig to the router table.) Rout both edges of each wheel. Reposition the jig and rout the smaller front tractor wheels.

Final Assembly

1. Cut a ⅜" dowel to 4¼" for the rear axle. Insert the rear axle through the tractor body and glue on the rear wheels. (We inserted 1" washers between the cab walls and wheels for smoother wheel movement and let the axles extend into wheel openings ¼".)

2. Cut a ¼"-diameter dowel to 4¼" for the front axle. Assemble the front wheels, this time using ½" washers.

3. Glue and clamp the fenders in place. (We first aligned the front edge of each fender with the front edge of the cab wall; then, we adjusted the back of each fender to have equal spacing between the wheels and fenders.)

4. Cut the stem on a toy axle peg to ¾". (We used a ⁷⁄₃₂ x 1⅛" peg available at wood supply and crafts stores, and mail order suppliers.) Glue it in the ⁷⁄₃₂" hole in the top of the body for the air cleaner. Cut a 1¼" piece of ¼" dowel. Now, sand a slight chamfer on one end and glue the opposite end in the exhaust pipe hole.

5. Finish-sand all parts and apply the finish of your choice. (We sprayed on two coats of clear polyurethane.)

Buying Guide
•**Maple stock.** ¼ x 7¼ x 24", catalog no. 4LU173; 1¾ x 7¼ x 24", catalog no. 4LU573. For current prices, contact Constantine, 2050 Eastchester Rd., Bronx, NY 10461, or call 800-223-8087.

Project Tool List
Tablesaw
Bandsaw
Router
    Router table
    ¼" round-over bit
Drill
Drill press
    Circle cutter
    Bits: ⁷⁄₃₂", ¼", ⁵⁄₁₆", ⅜", ⁷⁄₁₆"
Finishing sander

Note: *We built the project using the tools listed. You may be able to substitute other tools or equipment for listed items you don't have. Additional common tools and clamps may be required to complete the project.*

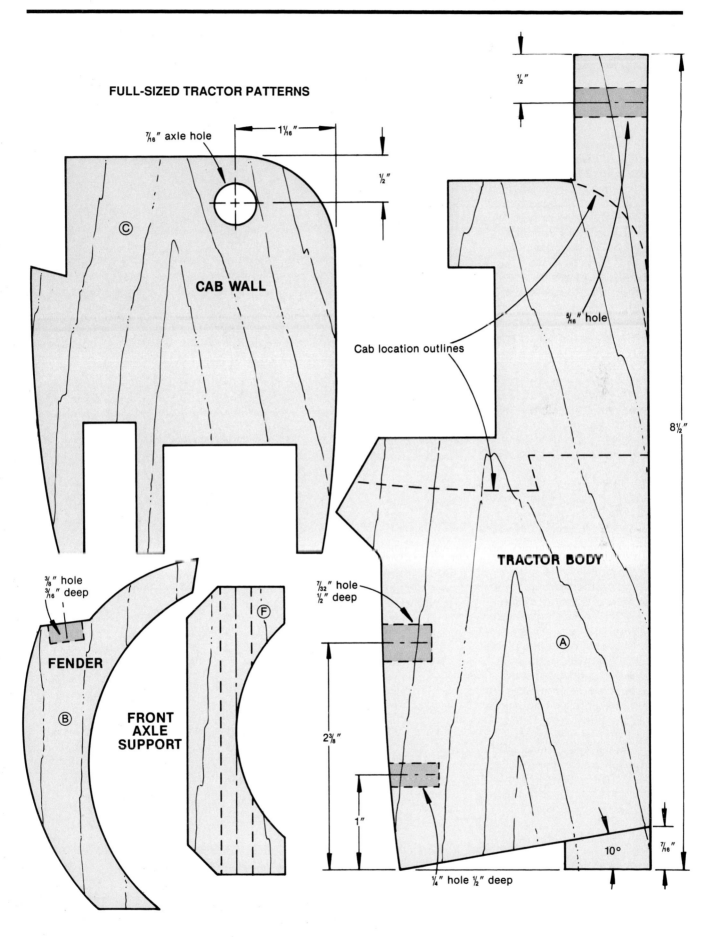

FULL-SIZED TRACTOR PATTERNS

$7/16''$ axle hole

$1^1/16''$

$1/2''$

Ⓒ

CAB WALL

$1/2''$

$5/16''$ hole

Cab location outlines

TRACTOR BODY

Ⓐ

$8^1/2''$

$7/32''$ hole
$1/2''$ deep

$3/8''$ hole
$3/16''$ deep

FENDER

Ⓕ

Ⓑ

**FRONT
AXLE
SUPPORT**

$2^3/8''$

$1''$

$10°$

$7/16''$

$1/4''$ hole $1/2''$ deep

63

SEA SKIPPER FOR YOUNG FLIERS

In hopes of making some young child happy, David Lanford, from Pipe Creek, Texas, entered this simple beauty in *WOOD*® magazine's 1991 Build-A-Toy™ contest. We like the floatplane because you can quickly cut the pieces to shape, and then fit them together like a puzzle.

1. Using a photocopy and spray adhesive or carbon paper, transfer the full-sized patterns *opposite* to ¼" plywood. (We chose Baltic birch because it's strong, smooth, and lacks voids.)

2. Check the thickness of your stock against the width of the marked notches (¼" plywood doesn't always measure exactly ¼" thick). Adjust the notch size if necessary for a snug fit, and cut the pieces to shape.

3. Drill a ⅟₁₆" hole through the center of the propeller.

4. Sand the pieces smooth (we progressed to 220-grit sandpaper), prime the pieces, mask off the mating surfaces for a good glue joint later, and then paint as desired. (We covered the mating surfaces with masking tape, sealed the plywood with two coats of aerosol lacquer, primed the pieces with white paint, and then used enamel modeling paints for the stripes. To form the straight lines, we used masking tape and painted one color at a time.)

5. Remove the masking tape, glue the parts together, and hold the propeller brad in the fuselage with instant glue. Don't use an accelerator with the instant glue; it will dissolve some paints.

Project Tool List
Scroll saw
Drill
  Bit: ⅟₁₆"
Finishing sander

EXPLODED VIEW

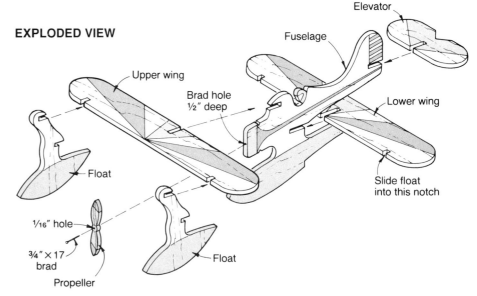

Upper wing

Brad hole ½" deep

Float

⅟₁₆" hole

¾" × 17 brad

Propeller

Fuselage

Elevator

Lower wing

Slide float into this notch

Float

Note: *We built the project using the tools listed. You may be able to substitute other tools or equipment for listed items you don't have.*

Additional common tools and clamps may be required to complete the project.

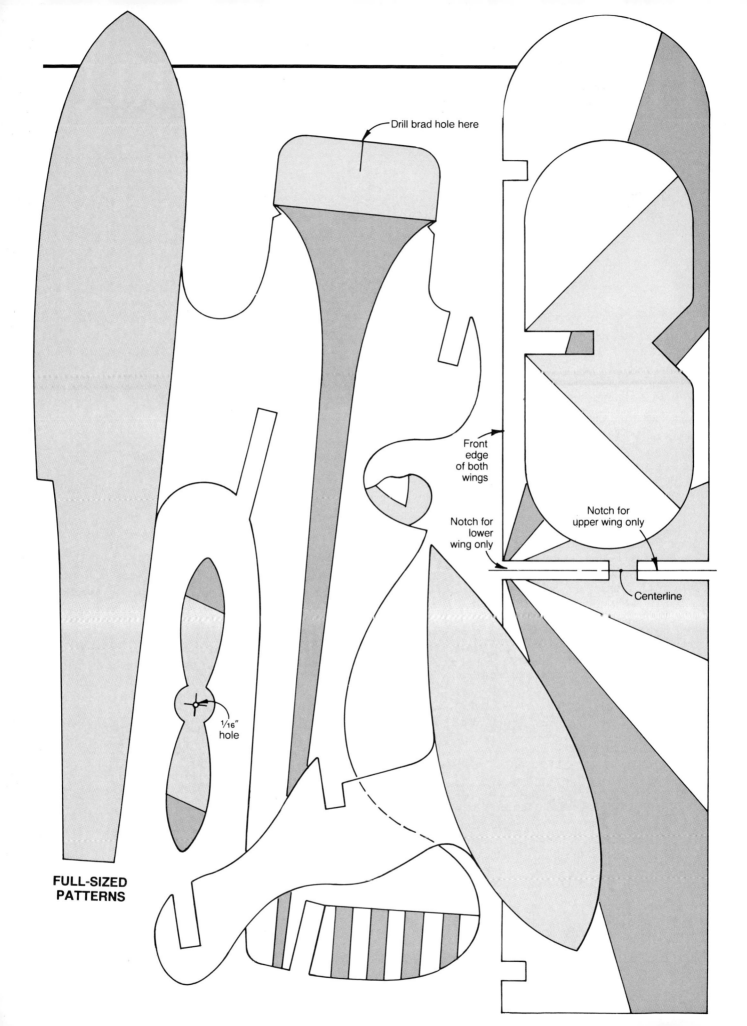

Drill brad hole here

Front edge of both wings

Notch for upper wing only

Notch for lower wing only

Centerline

1/16" hole

FULL-SIZED PATTERNS

IT'S A SMALL WORLD

Enter a magical world of small wonders, made large by the delight of a child who receives any one of these special gifts.

NOAH'S LOVABLE ARK

When family and friends see this great Noah's Ark and animals, they'll think you worked for 40 days and 40 nights. But thanks to our easy, pattern-packed plans, you can tell them it took less time to make than a rainy afternoon. Or, you could just keep 'em guessing!

You'll need these materials:

Build the ark with a 1×6"×4' pine board, a 12" length of 2×4, and a ¼" dowel at least 1" long. You'll need ¼" stock for the gangplank and the animals. Plane or resaw thicker stock to size. We used several wood species for the animals shown on the patterns.

First, let's build the ark

1. Cut four pieces of 1×6 pine 12" long. Now, make four photocopies of the full-sized Hull quarter

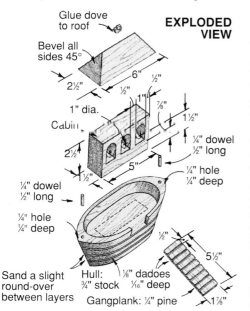

Glue dove to roof

EXPLODED VIEW

Bevel all sides 45°

2½" 6" ½"

½" 1" ⅞"

1" dia.

Cabin 1½"

2½" ¼" dowel ½" long

5" ¼" hole ¼" deep

¼" dowel ½" long

¼" hole ¼" deep

½"

Sand a slight round-over between layers

Hull: ¾" stock ⅛" dadoes ¹⁄₁₆" deep

Gangplank: ¼" pine

5½"

1⅞"

HULL LAYER DETAIL

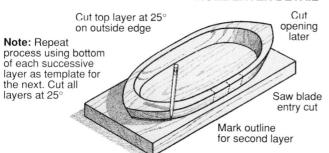

Cut top layer at 25° on outside edge

Note: Repeat process using bottom of each successive layer as template for the next. Cut all layers at 25°

Cut opening later

Saw blade entry cut

Mark outline for second layer

pattern on *page 68.* Scissor out the four sections, and then join them with cellophane tape to make a full-sized hull outline. Adhere the pattern to one of the hull pieces.

2. Next, tilt your bandsaw or scrollsaw table to 25°, and cut along the outside pattern line. Then, place the part you just cut with the narrow side down on top of another 1×6 piece. Trace the bottom outline as shown *bottom left,* and cut. Make four layers total, tracing each from the previous layer.

3. Now, return to the top (largest) layer and saw along the inside pattern line, entering the interior cut at the midpoint of the left side. *Do not cut inside the other hull layers.*

4. Finally, set the bandsaw table to 0°, and cut the gangplank opening 1⅞" wide, as shown on the Exploded View drawing *below left.* Sand round-overs on top and bottom edges of the hull layers (to create the grooved sides), apply glue, and clamp together. Once dry, drill a ¼" hole ¼" deep in each end where shown on the Exploded View drawing. Cut two pieces of ¼" dowel ½" long, apply glue, and insert.

5. Rip a 12" 2×4 to 2½". From this cut a 5" length for the cabin, and a 6" length for the roof. Next, bore three 1"-diameter holes through the cabin piece where shown on the Exploded View drawing. Cut the window bottoms with the scrollsaw. Adjust the bandsaw or scroll-saw table to 45°, and bevel the sides and ends of the 6" length to make the roof.

6. Saw ¼" stock to 1⅞"×5½" for the gangplank. With a tablesaw, cut ¹⁄₁₆"-deep blade kerfs ⅛" wide, spaced ½" apart on one side.

7. Sand off saw marks, and sand slight round-overs on the cabin and roof corners. Stain the deck, cabin, and gangplank. Paint as shown in the photo *opposite.*

8. For an aged look, scuff the

paint with sandpaper, sanding through to bare wood on some corners. Then, wipe with walnut stain. Now, glue together the hull, cabin, and roof.

And now, for the animals

1. Make two photocopies of each animal pattern, on *page 68.* For each, except the dove, cut three pieces of ¼"-thick stock to the dimensions shown on the pattern.

2. Laminate matched sets temporarily with double-faced tape. Use small pieces of tape so you can easily separate the pieces later.

3. Adhere a pattern to its respective stack. Then cut along the outermost line. Separate the three pieces. (If they don't come apart easily, dribble lacquer thinner into the joints to break the bond.)

4. Designate one piece the left side, one the right side, and one the center. Saw all legs off the *center* piece. Saw the head and tail from the *left* and *right* sides (but leave the tail on the crocodile's sides). Now, following the pattern lines, saw the extra legs off each side. Cut the elephant ears and tusks (we used pine for the tusks), and the lion ears. Cut the dove from a single thickness.

5. Assemble the animals, referring to the Animal Assembly detail. Round over the edges with sandpaper, and apply a clear finish. Glue the dove to the roof of Noah's ark.

Project Tool List

Tablesaw
Bandsaw
Scrollsaw
Drill press
 Bits: ¼", 1"
Finishing sander

Note: We built the project using the tools listed. You may be able to substitute other tools or equipment for listed items you don't have. Additional common tools and clamps may be required to complete the project.

continued

NOAH'S ARK
continued

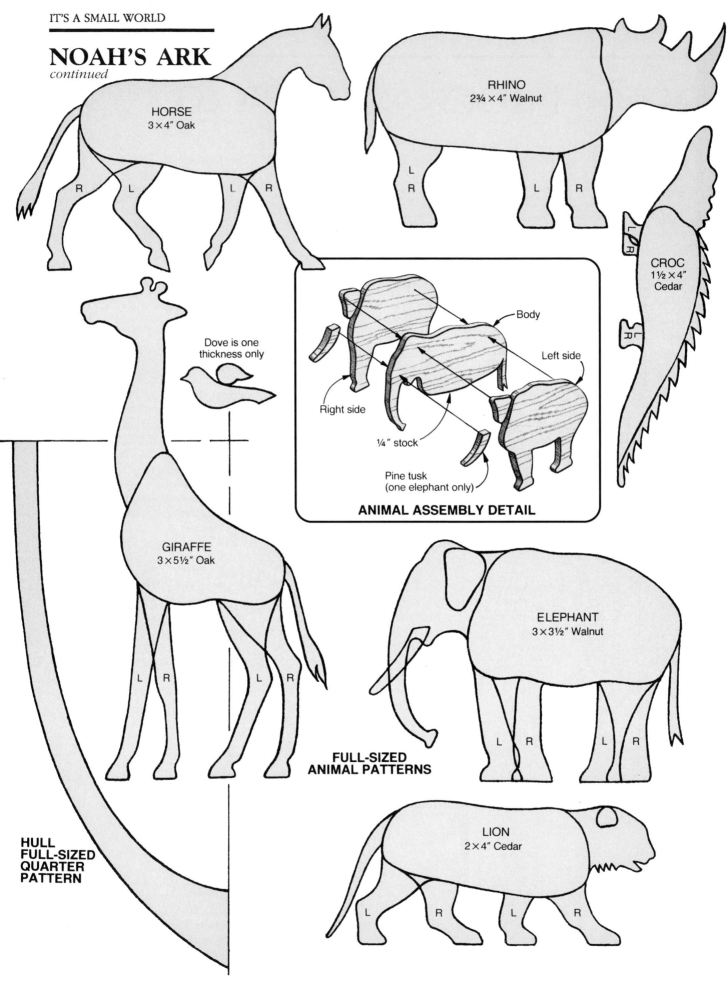

HORSE
3 × 4″ Oak

R L L R

RHINO
2¾ × 4″ Walnut

L R L R

CROC
1½ × 4″
Cedar

L R

L R

Dove is one
thickness only

Body

Left side

Right side

¼″ stock

Pine tusk
(one elephant only)

ANIMAL ASSEMBLY DETAIL

GIRAFFE
3 × 5½″ Oak

L R L R

ELEPHANT
3 × 3½″ Walnut

L R L R

**FULL-SIZED
ANIMAL PATTERNS**

**HULL
FULL-SIZED
QUARTER
PATTERN**

LION
2 × 4″ Cedar

L R L R

68

MILK TRUCK AND PICKUP

Truck body flush with the marked pattern lines.

3. Drill a pair of ⁹⁄₃₂" axle holes where located on the pattern.

4. Using a bandsaw fitted with a ⅛" blade, follow the pattern lines to cut the truck side profile to shape as shown in the photo *below left*.

5. Position the truck right side up, and mark the hood and radiator lines where dimensioned on the Top View drawing on *page 71*. Cut the front of the truck to shape on the bandsaw as shown in the photo *below*.

Form the recess for the front-wheel spacers

1. Chuck a ⅝" flat-bottomed bit (we used a Forstner bit) into your drill press. (The recommended speed for a ⅝" Forstner bit in softwood is 2,400 rpm.)

2. Position the truck body on its side on the drill-press table. Center the bit over the previously drilled front-axle hole, and clamp the truck body firmly to the drill-press table with a handscrew clamp. Now, as shown in the photo on *page 70 left*, start the drill, and bore a ¹⁄₁₆"-deep hole. (The area bored with the flat-bottomed bit should be flush with the motor sides cut with the bandsaw.) Remove the clamp, flip the truck body over, and repeat the centering, clamping, and drilling operation on the other side.

continued

Start to finish, it won't take you more than an evening or two **to build these delightful pint-sized vehicles. Whether you use them as country decorations or present them to a lucky child as a gift, you can count on these trucks being a big hit.**

Note: The following directions are for the milk truck. We built the pick-up nearly identically except for the pickup box and rear-wheel spacers. See the drawing on page 70 for alter-ations when building the pickup.

Cut the chassis to shape

1. Cut a knot-free 12" length from a pine, fir, or spruce 2x6. Plane or joint one edge (not a face) to remove the rounded corners. Crosscut the 12" length in half. You'll need one 6" length now for the milk truck body (A) and the other one later if you decide to build the pickup body (B).

2. Using carbon paper or a photocopy machine, transfer the full-sized Side View Milk Truck pattern on *page 71* to white paper. Apply spray-on adhesive to the back of the paper pattern. Apply the Side View pattern to one of your 6"-long blocks, with the *top* of the pattern flush with the *planed* edge of the block. Now, crosscut the front and back of the Milk

Square the blade with the table, and cut the truck body profile to shape on a bandsaw fitted with a ⅛" blade.

Carefully mark the two hood layout lines, and cut the truck front to shape on the bandsaw.

MILK TRUCK AND PICKUP
continued

3. Remove the paper pattern, and sand the truck body smooth. (Lacquer thinner works great for dissolving the adhesive and releasing the paper pattern.)

Shape and attach the fenders and seat

1. To form the fenders (D), start by crosscutting a 12" length from a 2×4. Plane one edge (not a face) to remove the rounded corners. Position the rip fence on your tablesaw ¼" from the inside edge of the saw blade. Now, rip the planed edge from the 2×4 for a piece measuring ¼"×1½"×12". Reposition the fence, and rip the 1½"-wide piece to a 1" width.

2. Transfer the full-sized fender pattern twice to the face of the stock, and bandsaw two fenders from the 12"-long piece.

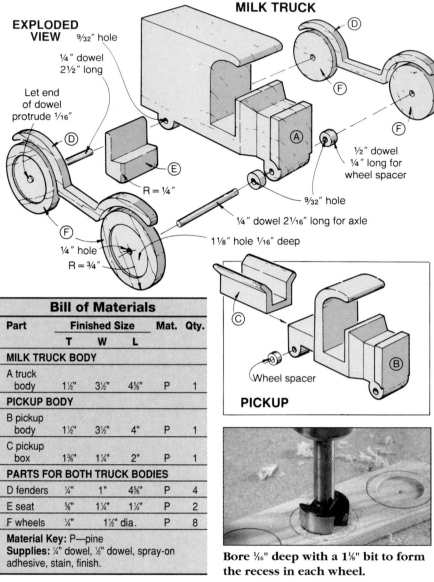

MILK TRUCK

EXPLODED VIEW

9/32" hole

¼" dowel
2½" long

Let end of dowel protrude 1/16"

R = ¼"

R = ¾"

¼" hole

½" dowel ¼" long for wheel spacer

9/32" hole

¼" dowel 2 1/16" long for axle

1 1/8" hole 1/16" deep

Wheel spacer

PICKUP

Finish forming the wheel-spacer recess with a flat-bottomed bit.

Part	Finished Size			Mat.	Qty.
	T	**W**	**L**		
MILK TRUCK BODY					
A truck body	1½"	3½"	4⅝"	P	1
PICKUP BODY					
B pickup body	1½"	3½"	4"	P	1
C pickup box	1⅜"	1¼"	2"	P	1
PARTS FOR BOTH TRUCK BODIES					
D fenders	¼"	1"	4⅝"	P	4
E seat	⅝"	1¼"	1¼"	P	2
F wheels	¼"		1½" dia.	P	8

Material Key: P—pine
Supplies: ¼" dowel, ½" dowel, spray-on adhesive, stain, finish.

3. Sand the fenders smooth. Glue and clamp the fenders to the side of the truck body. (Make sure the bottom edge of the truck body and fenders align where shown on the drawing *opposite*.)

4. Bandsaw a piece of 2×4 material to ⅝" thick by 1½" wide by 1¼" long for the seat (E). Transfer the full-sized side profile *opposite* to the end of the block, and cut the seat to shape on the bandsaw. Sand a ¼" round-over on the front corners of the seat.

Now, add the wheels

1. Cut a piece of pine stock to ¼"×2½"×12" (we resawed a section of 2×4 material to size). Using a compass, mark four 1½"-diameter circles on one face of the stock. When marking the circles, push hard on the compass point to make a small indentation in the wood.

2. Chuck a 1⅛" flat-bottomed bit into your drill press. Center the bit over the centerpoint of one of the circles, and drill a 1/16"-deep recess as shown in the photo *above right*. (We set the depth stop on our drill press to ensure that all recesses would be the same depth.)

3. Cut the wheels to shape. You can use a circle cutter to shape the wheels on the drill press, or use a bandsaw or scrollsaw.

Bore 1/16" deep with a 1⅛" bit to form the recess in each wheel.

4. From ½" dowel stock, cut two pieces ¼" long for the wheel spacers. Clamp each spacer in a small handscrew clamp, and drill a 9/32" hole in the center of each.

5. Cut two pieces of ¼" dowel stock to 2 1/16" long for the truck axles.

You're almost ready to hit the road

1. Sand all the pieces smooth, and stain them as desired.

2. To add the sign, transfer the full-sized "MILK" logo onto heavy white paper, and carefully cut it to shape (we used a hobby knife). Color the sign with marking pencils if desired. Spray the back of the pattern with spray-on adhesive, and stick the logo to the truck body.

3. Apply the finish to all the pieces, except for the axles. (We sprayed on a lacquer finish.) Covering the MILK logo with finish will help protect it over time.

4. Glue one wheel to each axle so the wooden axle protrudes 1/16" beyond the wheel where shown on the Exploded View drawing.

5. After the glue dries, slide the back axle and wheel assembly through the rear axle hole, and glue on the other wheel. For the front axle, slide on a wheel spacer, and slide the axle through the truck, slip on another wheel spacer, and then glue on the other wheel.

Tips on building the pickup

Now that you've mastered the milk truck construction, try your hand at building our closely related pickup. To do this, transfer the pickup-body outline shown on the full-sized patterns at *right* to the piece of 2x6 stock cut in Step 1 under the heading "Cut the chassis to shape."

When bandsawing the pickup body to shape, cut the box portion from the truck body where marked with dashed lines on the full-sized side view pattern. Using the full-sized Box drawing (*above right*), bandsaw the box to shape, hand-sand smooth, and glue it onto the pickup chassis. As shown on the Exploded View drawing of the pickup *opposite*, you'll need to form two rear-wheel spacers to prevent the back wheels from rubbing against the sides of the pickup box.

Project Tool List
Tablesaw
Bandsaw
Jointer
Drill press
   Circle cutter
   Bits: 1/4", 9/32", 5/8"
Finishing sander

Note: *We built the project using the tools listed. You may be able to substitute other tools or equipment for listed items you don't have. Additional common tools and clamps may be required to complete the project.*

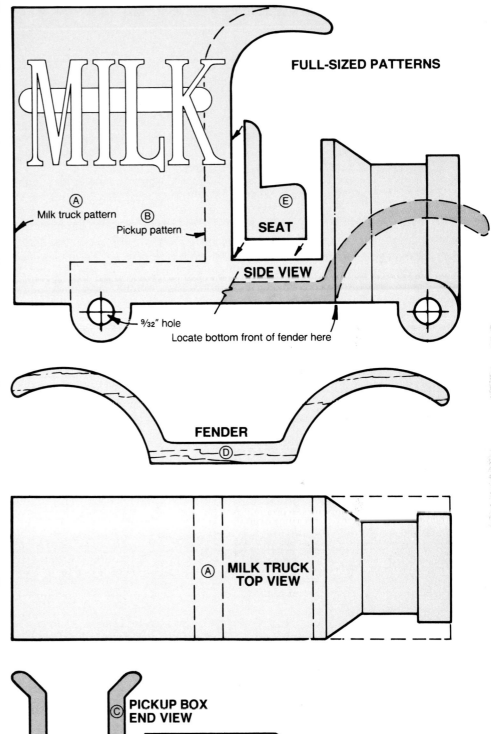

FULL-SIZED PATTERNS

Ⓐ Milk truck pattern   Ⓑ Pickup pattern

Ⓔ SEAT

SIDE VIEW

9/32" hole

Locate bottom front of fender here

FENDER   Ⓓ

Ⓐ MILK TRUCK TOP VIEW

Ⓒ PICKUP BOX END VIEW

Ⓑ PICKUP TOP VIEW

TINY TYKE TOOLBOX 'N' TOOLS

Most kids can't resist the urge to give Mom and Dad a helping hand. But, too often, children lack the tools to turn an imaginary screw or pound a block of wood. Not any longer! Now you can turn your budding builders loose with our wooden tools and toolbox designed and built just for them.

Let's start with the toolbox

1. To make the toolbox ends (A), cut two pieces of ¾" stock to 6x7¼". Cut the sides (B) to the size listed in the Bill of Materials. With double-faced tape, stick the ends together face-to-face with the edges and ends flush. Then, stick the sides together.

2. Using the dimensions on the Toolbox drawing *below,* mark the hole centerpoints on the top face of the taped-together ends and sides.

3. Drill 1" holes in the ends and sides where marked. Switch bits and drill the ⁷⁄₁₆" hole through the ends. Now, with a ¼" bit, drill the holes through the sides.

4. Mark the cutlines on the end pieces. Bandsaw the angled lines.

5. With a wood wedge, pry the pieces apart, and remove the tape.

6. Cut or rout a ⅛" groove ¼" deep ¼" from the bottom inside edge in the side and end pieces. Then, form a ¾" rabbet ¼" deep across the ends of the side pieces.

7. Rout a ⅛" round-over along the end and side pieces where shown on the Toolbox drawing. (We used our table-mounted router to rout the round-overs.)

8. Cut the bottom (C) to size (we used ⅛" birch plywood).

9. Dry-clamp the parts (A, B, C) to check the fit. Glue and clamp the box, checking for square. Later, use the previously drilled ¼" holes in the box sides as guides to drill ¼" holes ⁹⁄₁₆" deep into the edges of the ends. Put a drop of glue in each hole and plug the holes with ¼" axle pegs.

10. Cut the handle (D) to length from a ¾" dowel. (We left a ¹⁄₁₆" gap between the axle peg and end pieces so the handle will rotate.) Drill a ⅜" hole ¾" deep centered in each end of the handle. Put a drop of glue in the holes, and pin the handle to the box with ⅜" axle pegs. Finish-sand the box and add the finish.

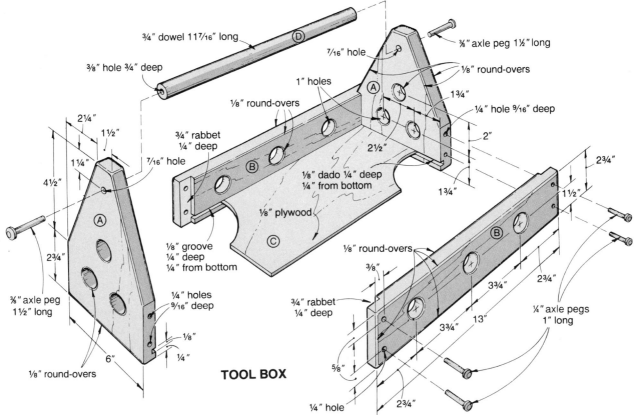

TOOL BOX

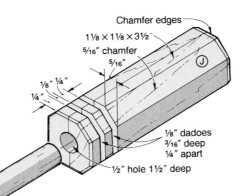

Chamfer edges

1⅛" × 1⅛" × 3½"

5/16" chamfer

5/16"

⅛" ¼"

¼"

J

⅛" dadoes
3/16" deep
¼" apart

½" hole 1½" deep

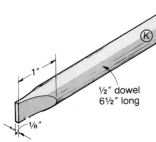

K

1"

½" dowel
6½" long

⅛"

The screwdriver adds to the set

1. To form the handle (J), plane a 1⅛"-wide by 12"-long piece of ¾"-thick walnut stock to 5/16" thick. Crosscut the piece in half. Glue the two pieces face-to-face with the edges and ends flush.

Bill of Materials					
Part	**Finished Size**			**Mat.**	**Qty.**
	T	**W**	**L**		
TOOL BOX					
A ends	¾"	6"	7¼"	O	2
B sides	¾"	2¾"	13"	O	2
C bottom	⅛"	6"	12"	BP	1
D handle	¾" dia.		11¹¹⁄₁₆"	D	1
SAW					
E handle	¾"	3½"	6"	W	1
F blade	⅛"	2"	8½"	BP	1
SQUARE					
G handle	¾"	1⅞"	4⅛"	W	1
H blade	⅛"	1½"	6"	BP	1
PLIERS					
I handle blank	¾"	3"	7¾"	W	1
SCREWDRIVER					
J handle	1⅛"	1⅛"	3½"	LW	1
K blade	½" dia.		6½"	D	1
MALLET					
L head	1½"	1½"	4"	LW	1
M handle	¾" dia.		9¼"	D	1

Material Key: O–oak, BP–birch plywood, D–dowel stock, W–walnut, LW–laminated walnut.
Supplies: double-faced tape, ⅜" axle pegs 1½" long, ¼" axle pegs 1" long, finish.

2. Crosscut one end for a flat surface. Draw diagonals on the cut end to find center, and drill a ½" hole 1½" deep into the handle.

3. Cut 5/16" chamfers along all four corners of the handle. Crosscut the end opposite the ½" hole.

4. To cut the handle kerfs, raise the tablesaw blade ⅛" above the table. Attach an auxiliary fence and stop to your miter gauge. Mark the kerf locations on the handle. Place the handle against the auxiliary fence, align the marks with the blade, position the stop, start the saw, and rotate the handle to cut the kerf. Reset the stop, and cut the second kerf.

HANDSAW

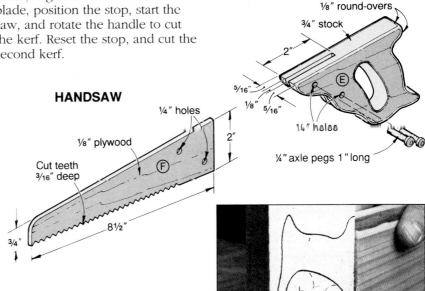

¼" holes

⅛" plywood

Cut teeth
3/16" deep

F

2"

¾"

8½"

5. Sand a slight chamfer on the handle ends.

6. To form the blade (K), cut a 6½" length of ½" dowel. Belt-sand one end to the shape shown, and glue the other in the handle.

Now, saw the saw

1. Cut a piece of ¾" walnut to 3½" wide by 6" long for the handsaw handle (E).

2. Using carbon paper or a photocopy and spray adhesive,

transfer the full-sized handsaw handle pattern to the walnut, including the hole centerpoints.

3. As shown in the photo *below,* cut a ⅛" kerf 2" deep in the blade end of the handle.

4. Drill the ¼" holes for the pegs and 1⅛" holes for the opening.

5. With a scrollsaw or coping saw, cut between the two 1⅛" holes to finish forming the opening. Cut the handle to shape. Sand the opening smooth with a 1" sanding drum.

6. Rout ⅛" round-overs on the handle where shown on *page 74.*

7. Lay out the saw-blade outline on a piece of ⅛×2×8½" birch plywood for part F. Use the full-sized tooth pattern to mark the teeth outline along one edge. Cut the blade and teeth to shape (we used a bandsaw). Sand the teeth smooth to dull the sharp points.

continued

⅛" round-overs

¾" stock

2"

E

5/16"

⅛" 5/16"

¼" holes

¼" axle pegs 1" long

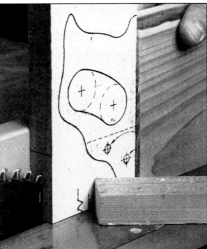

Use a push block to safely feed the handle blank over the tablesaw blade.

TINY TYKE TOOLBOX 'N' TOOLS
continued

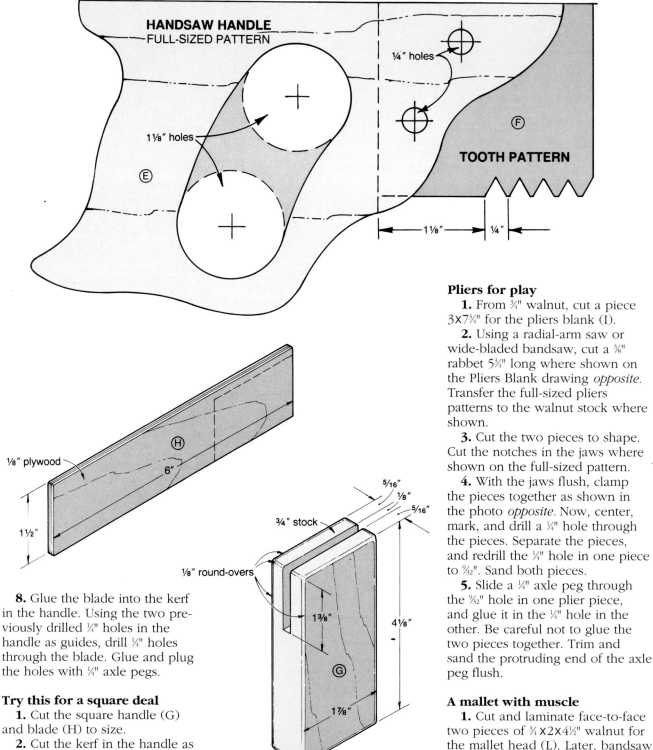

HANDSAW HANDLE
FULL-SIZED PATTERN

¼" holes

1⅛" holes

Ⓔ

Ⓕ

TOOTH PATTERN

1⅛" ¼"

⅛" plywood

Ⓗ

6"

1½"

¾" stock

5/16"
⅛"
5/16"

⅛" round-overs

1⅜"

4⅛"

Ⓖ

1⅞"

8. Glue the blade into the kerf in the handle. Using the two previously drilled ¼" holes in the handle as guides, drill ¼" holes through the blade. Glue and plug the holes with ¼" axle pegs.

Try this for a square deal
1. Cut the square handle (G) and blade (H) to size.
2. Cut the kerf in the handle as you did earlier with the handsaw handle. Rout the edges of the handle and glue the blade in place

Pliers for play
1. From ¾" walnut, cut a piece 3×7¾" for the pliers blank (I).
2. Using a radial-arm saw or wide-bladed bandsaw, cut a ⅜" rabbet 5¾" long where shown on the Pliers Blank drawing *opposite*. Transfer the full-sized pliers patterns to the walnut stock where shown.
3. Cut the two pieces to shape. Cut the notches in the jaws where shown on the full-sized pattern.
4. With the jaws flush, clamp the pieces together as shown in the photo *opposite*. Now, center, mark, and drill a ¼" hole through the pieces. Separate the pieces, and redrill the ¼" hole in one piece to 9/32". Sand both pieces.
5. Slide a ¼" axle peg through the 9/32" hole in one plier piece, and glue it in the ¼" hole in the other. Be careful not to glue the two pieces together. Trim and sand the protruding end of the axle peg flush.

A mallet with muscle
1. Cut and laminate face-to-face two pieces of ¾×2×4½" walnut for the mallet head (L). Later, bandsaw the lamination to the shape shown on the Mallet drawing *opposite*.

With the notched jaws flush, clamp the plier pieces together, and drill the ¼" peg hole (we used a brad-point bit).

2. Mark the centerpoint location, and drill a ¾" hole 1" deep into the mallet head. Cut a ¾"-diameter piece of dowel stock to 9¼" long for the handle (M). Glue the handle into the mallet head.

Project Tool List
Tablesaw
   Dado blade or dado set
Bandsaw
Scrollsaw
Belt sander
Router
   Router table
   Bits: ⅛" straight, ⅛" round-over
Drill press
   Sanding drum
   Bits: ¼", ⁹⁄₃₂", ⅜", ⁷⁄₁₆", ½", ¾", 1"
Finishing sander

Note: *We built the project using the tools listed. You may be able to substitute other tools or equipment for listed items you don't have. Additional common tools and clamps may be required to complete the project.*

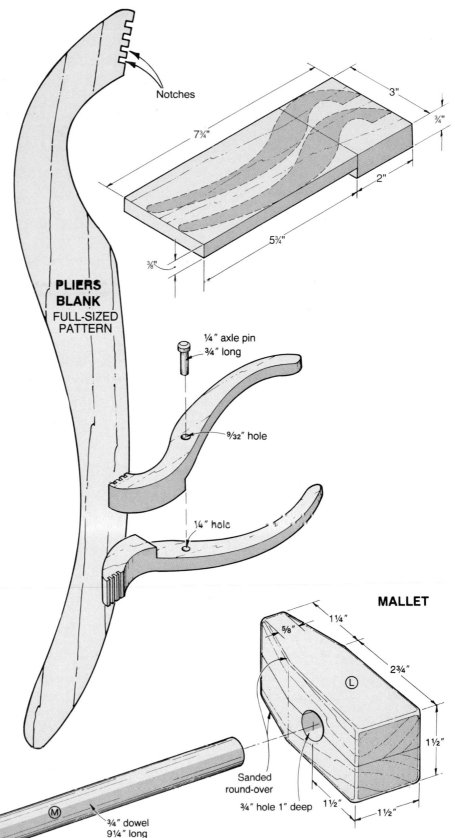

Notches

PLIERS BLANK
FULL-SIZED PATTERN

¼" axle pin
¾" long

⁹⁄₃₂" hole

¼" hole

7¾"
3"
¾"
2"
5¾"
⅜"

MALLET

1¼"
⅝"
2¾"
Ⓛ
1½"
Sanded round-over
¾" hole 1" deep
1½"
1½"

Round-over end
Ⓜ
¾" dowel 9¼" long

BARBIE'S DREAMWORLD

Here's a piece scaled for Mattel's popular Barbie® and other 10"- to 13"-tall fashion dolls. This diminutive bed will be a big hit with doll fanciers of all ages and can be matched with the armoire project that begins on *page 90*.

We'll cut the parts first

Note: This project requires ½"-thick hardwood stock for the bed posts and ¼" material for the other bed frame parts. As shown on the Cutting diagram opposite, we started with a ½ X 5½ X 24" piece of stock. After removing the ½ X ½ X 15" strip for the posts, we planed the remaining piece to ¼" thick.

1. Turn the ½" thick piece (we used cherry) on edge, and cut a ⅛"-wide kerf ⅛" deep where dimensioned on the Post detail

opposite. Next, set your saw's rip fence ½" from the inside of the saw blade and rip the grooved strip from the cherry stock. From this strip, crosscut two 4" lengths for the head posts (A), and two 3¼" lengths for the foot posts (B).

Note: To safely cut the small parts on our tablesaw, we made a wood table insert and elevated the blade up through it. We also used feather boards and a pushstick when ripping thin stock.

2. From ¼" cherry, rip and crosscut one 3¾ X 7¼" piece for the headboard (C), and one 2¼ X 7¼" piece for the footboard (D). From the same stock, rip and crosscut two 1 X 12¼" pieces for the side rails (E). Cut four ¾ X ¾" post caps (F). If your planer doesn't dress stock this thin, adhere it with double-faced tape to a larger piece of wood, and

pass both through your planer. Or, resaw the stock on a bandsaw or tablesaw.

3. From ½" plywood, cut the box spring (G) to the size listed on the Bill of Materials *opposite*. Now, finish-sand all of the parts, using 150- and 220-grit sandpaper.

4. Glue and clamp the side rails to the long edges of the box spring, aligning the bottom edges of the rails and the box spring. (We used yellow woodworker's glue.) When dry, lay out a ⅛ X ⅜" notch in each corner for the posts as shown on the Corner detail. Saw the notches.

Next, shape the headboard

1. Make a copy of the Router Template pattern and Headboard pattern on *page 79*. (We photocopied ours.) Cut a 4 X 8" piece of plywood that's slightly thicker than

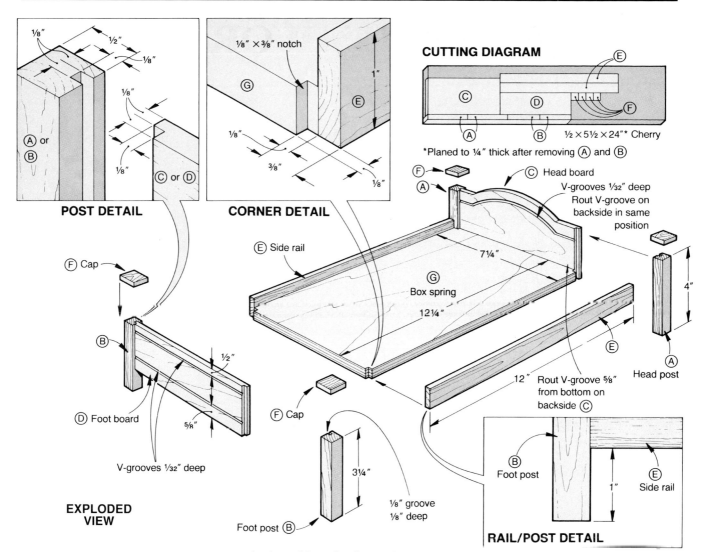

POST DETAIL

1/8" 1/2" 1/8"

A or B

C or D

CORNER DETAIL

1/8" × 3/8" notch

G

E

1"

1/8"

3/8"

1/8"

CUTTING DIAGRAM

E

C

D

F

A

B

1/2 × 5½ × 24"* Cherry

*Planed to ¼" thick after removing A and B

F

A

C Head board
V-grooves 1/32" deep
Rout V-groove on
backside in same
position

7¼"

G
Box spring

12¼"

4"

E

A
Head post

12" Rout V-groove 5/8"
from bottom on
backside C

E Side rail

F Cap

B

D Foot board

1/2"

5/8"

V-grooves 1/32" deep

**EXPLODED
VIEW**

F Cap

Foot post B

3¼"

1/8" groove
1/8" deep

B
Foot post

1"

E
Side rail

RAIL/POST DETAIL

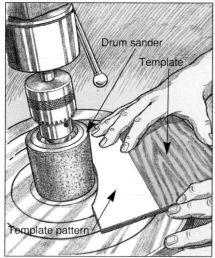

Drum sander

Template

Template pattern

the barrel length of your ¾" O.D. router bushing. (The barrel on ours measured 9/16" long, so we used 5/8" thick plywood. For a source of router bushings, see the Buying Guide.) Adhere the Router template pattern to the plywood (we used spray adhesive), aligning it along the front edge and sides. Scrollsaw the curve, cutting just outside the line. Now, sand to the line with a drum sander as shown at *left*.

2. Clamp a piece of scrap approximately 12×15" to the top of your workbench, and place the headboard on it. Locate and scribe a faint vertical centerline on the headboard face. Next, position the template on the headboard, aligning the centerline and the front edge of the template 1" down from the top of the headboard. Nail them together where instructed, with *continued*

Bill of Materials				
Part	**Finished Size**		**Mat.**	**Qty.**
	T	**W**	**L**		
A head posts	½"	½"	4"	C	2
B foot posts	½"	½"	3¼"	C	2
C headboard	¼"	3¾"	7¼"	C	1
D footboard	¼"	2¼"	7¼"	C	1
E side rail	¼"	1"	12"	C	2
F cap	¼"	¾"	¾"	C	4
G box spring	½"	7¼"	12¼"	P	1

Material Key: C–cherry, P–plywood
Supplies: ½ X 7¼ X 12¼ " foam; 9 X 27" fabric for mattress cover; finish.

BARBIE'S DREAMWORLD
continued

brads long enough to penetrate into the scrap. If you nail where indicated on the template you'll cut away the nail holes later.

3. Attach a ¾" O.D. router bushing to your router's baseplate and chuck a 60° V-groove bit into the collet. Set the bit depth so it cuts a 1⁄32"-deep groove. Next, place the router's baseplate on the template, push the bushing against the front edge of the template, and rout from left to right to cut the arched groove as shown at *right*. (With double-faced tape, we placed a 5⁄8" spacer to the headboard to help support the router.) Remove the template, nail it to the backside of the headboard, and using the same procedures, rout the arching groove on that face.

4. Mount your router in a router table, and using a fence, rout straight grooves where indicated across the front face of the footboard and on the headboard back.

5. With your tablesaw, cut ⅛x⅛" rabbets on the edges of the headboard and footboard where shown on the Exploded View drawing. Next, adhere the headboard pattern to the headboard, and scrollsaw the top to shape as shown at *right*. (We sawed just wide of the line, then sanded to the line.) Remove the pattern.

6. Using the Exploded View drawing for reference, dry-assemble the bed to test the fit of each part. Adjust part dimensions if necessary. Glue the foot posts to the footboard and clamp. Glue and clamp the head posts to the headboard. Check the assemblies for square. Wipe off glue squeeze-out with a damp cloth.

7. Glue and clamp the footboard and headboard assemblies to the box spring, aligning the bottom of the box spring flush with the bottom edges of the headboard and footboard. Check for square. Center and glue a cap to the top of each post, and clamp lightly.

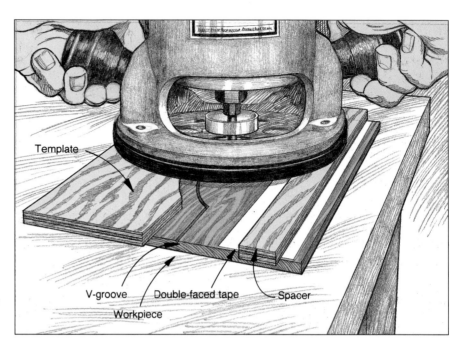

Template
V-groove
Workpiece
Double-faced tape
Spacer

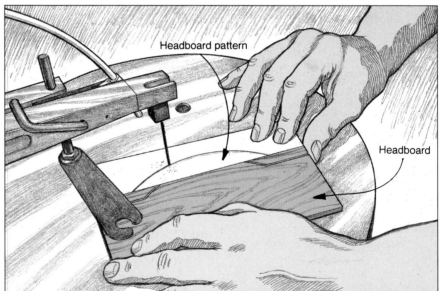

Headboard pattern
Headboard

Now, the final touches

1. Apply the finish. (We wiped on a cherry stain and let it dry thoroughly. Next, we applied one coat of water-based lacquer sanding sealer, and then two coats of waterbased lacquer, sanding between coats with 220-grit sandpaper.)

2. For the mattress, cut a piece of 1"-thick foam to fit inside the bed rails. Follow the instructions on the Mattress Cover detail *opposite* to sew a cloth mattress cover.

Buying Guide

• **¾" O.D. Router Bushing.** Fits most routers; adaptors available for others. Bushing, catalog no. 04I33. Requires 04C44 lock nut. For current prices, contact Woodcraft Supply Corp., P.O. Box 1686,

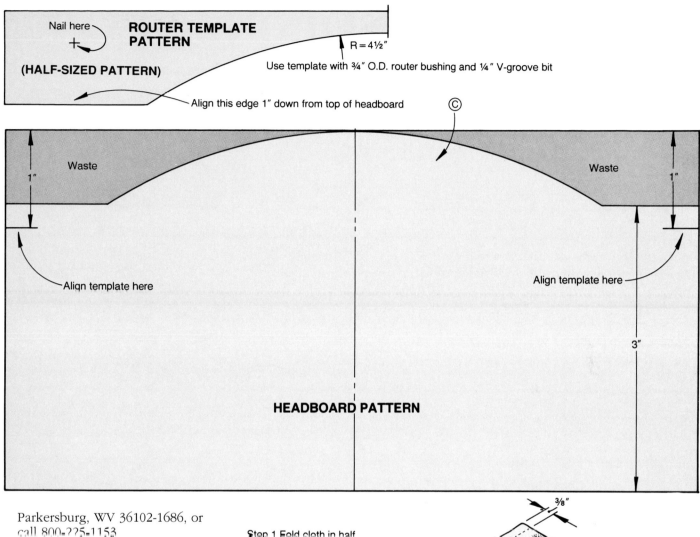

ROUTER TEMPLATE PATTERN

Nail here

(HALF-SIZED PATTERN)

R = 4½"

Use template with ¾" O.D. router bushing and ¼" V-groove bit

Align this edge 1" down from top of headboard

ⓒ

Waste

1"

Waste

1"

Align template here

Align template here

3"

HEADBOARD PATTERN

Parkersburg, WV 36102-1686, or
call 800-225-1153

BARBIE trademark and ® 1993 by
Mattel, Inc. Used with permission.
BARBIE® doll shown for illustration
only. This bed plan not connected
with Mattel, Inc.

Project Tool List
Tablesaw
Planer
Drill press
  Sanding drum
Router
  ¾" bushing
  V-groove bit
Finishing sander

Note: *We built the project using
the tools listed. You may be able to
substitute other tools or equipment
for listed items you don't have.
Additional common tools and
clamps may be required to
complete the project.*

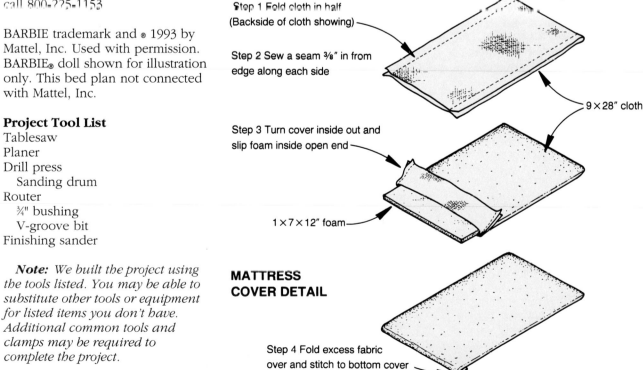

3/8"

Step 1 Fold cloth in half
(Backside of cloth showing)

Step 2 Sew a seam 3/8" in from
edge along each side

9 × 28" cloth

Step 3 Turn cover inside out and
slip foam inside open end

1 × 7 × 12" foam

**MATTRESS
COVER DETAIL**

Step 4 Fold excess fabric
over and stitch to bottom cover

TEA-FOR-TWO DINING SET

We let a wide-eyed girl of seven years try our table and chairs to entertain a few of her stuffed animals. A little later, we had to beg her to return the dining set in order to photograph it. We fashioned the set from oak and applied a pleasing honey-colored finish. Use our full-sized patterns for quick, quality results.

Note: We used ½"-thick oak. One table and one chair requires three 7¼x36" boards. Add a second 7½x24" board and scrap piece for each additional chair. You can plane thicker stock or purchase it. (See the Buying Guide for our source.)

Begin with the chair

1. Using a photocopier or carbon paper, make three copies of the full-sized chair and table patterns on *page 83.* Include the center-points for the pegs and dowels.

2. Adhere the Chair Side Pattern (A) to a piece of ¼" hardboard. Cut the hardboard to shape (we

used a scrollsaw), sawing just outside the line, and then sanding to the line.

Note: We cut the chair sides to shape with a router. If you prefer to cut out the parts with a scrollsaw, adhere or trace the pattern directly onto the ½" stock, and then saw the parts to shape. Stack-cut and sand the parts.

3. Drill the four ⅛" holes in the chair side template, and counter-sink two of them. Lay the template on your ½"-oak stock, and, using a self-centering punch, mark the four holes. Drill the ⅛" holes.

4. Drive two 1¼"-long drywall screws through the countersunk holes in the template, the ½" oak, and into a piece of scrap plywood that can be clamped to a bench.

5. Mount a ⁵⁄₁₆" guide bushing and a ¼" straight bit to your router. Adjust the router so it cuts through the ½" oak in two passes. Rout the chair side and arm opening, as shown *above right,* letting the guide bushing follow the template. Remove the screws and template, and enlarge the ⅛" holes to ¼".

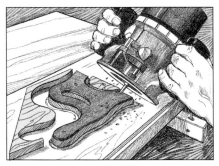

6. To make the second chair side, repeat Steps 3, 4, and 5. If you want more than one chair, make the required number of sides at this time.

Make the remaining chair parts

1. To make the chair seat (B), seat support (C), and headrest (D), rip and crosscut a piece of ½" oak to 4x7½". (See the Cutting Diagram *opposite.*)

2. From this, rip one chair seat 3½x4"; one seat support 1x4"; and one headrest 1½x4".

3. Next, apply the patterns to the seat support and headrest.

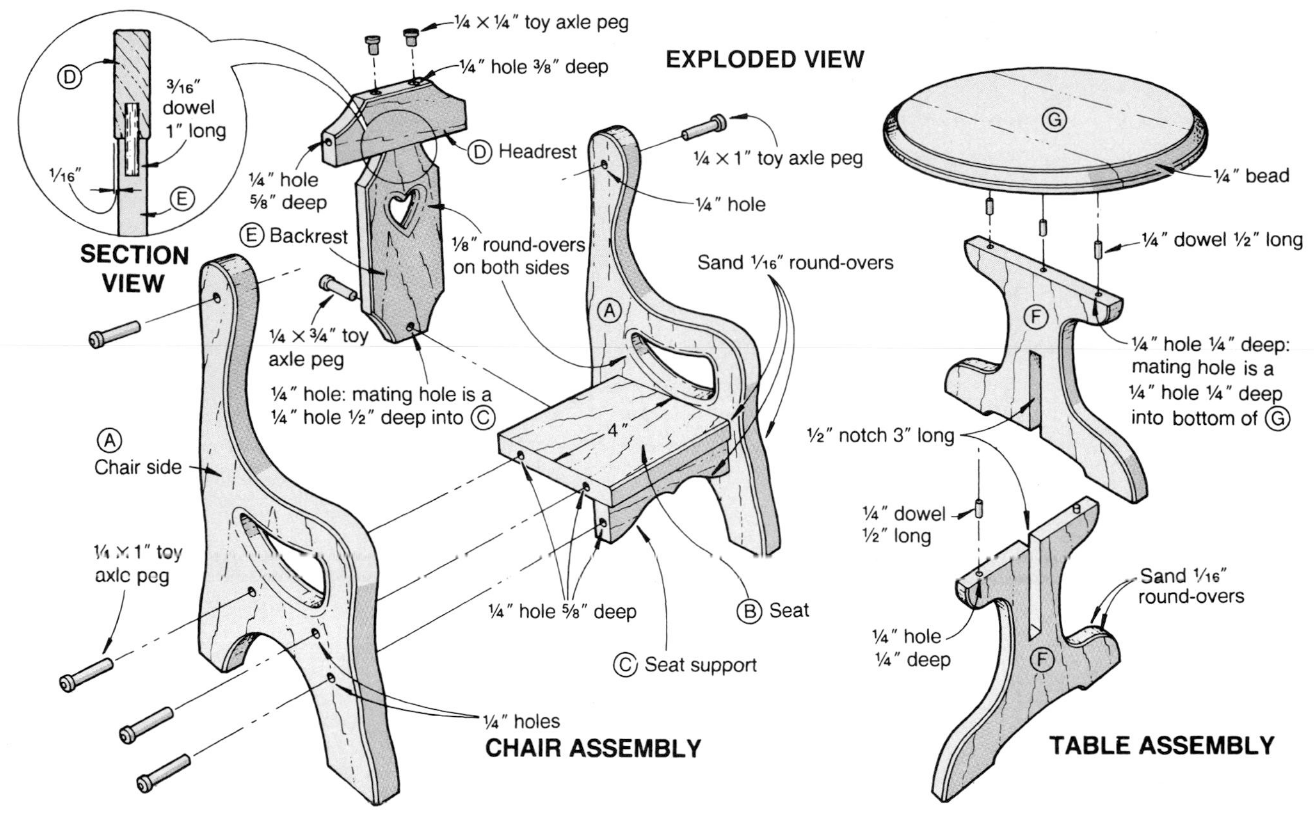
¼ × ¼" toy axle peg
¼" hole ⅜" deep
EXPLODED VIEW
D
3/16" dowel 1" long
1/16"
E
SECTION VIEW
¼" hole ⅝" deep
D Headrest
E Backrest
⅛" round-overs on both sides
¼ × 1" toy axle peg
¼" hole
Sand 1/16" round-overs
G
¼" bead
¼" dowel ½" long
F
¼ × ¾" toy axle peg
¼" hole: mating hole is a ¼" hole ½" deep into C
A
A Chair side
4"
¼" hole ¼" deep: mating hole is a ¼" hole ¼" deep into bottom of G
½" notch 3" long
¼" dowel ½" long
¼ × 1" toy axle peg
¼" hole ⅝" deep
B Seat
C Seat support
Sand 1/16" round-overs
¼" hole ¼" deep
F
¼" holes
CHAIR ASSEMBLY
TABLE ASSEMBLY

4. For the chair's backrest (E), trace the full-sized pattern and the heart opening onto a piece of ⅜"-thick oak stock.

5. Cut the parts (C), (D), and (E) to final shape on a scrollsaw. Cut wide of the line, and sand to the line with a drum sander. Drill a blade start hole through the heart opening in the backrest, thread the scrollsaw blade through the hole, and cut the heart opening to shape.

6. Using the dimensions on the full-sized patterns on *page 83* and the Chair Assembly draw-ing *above* for the chair, mark the locations of all the screw holes on each piece. Next, drill all of the holes. (We used a self-centering doweling jig to ensure the holes would be drilled straight.)

7. Chuck a ⅛" round-over bit in your table-mounted router and round over both edges of the heart in the chair back, and the opening in the chair sides. Hand-sand slight round-overs along the edges on the other chair parts. Finally, finish-sand all parts.

Bill of Materials

Part	Finished Size T	W	L	Mat.	Qty.
A sides	½"	5⅝"	9⅜"	O	2
B seat	½"	3½"	4"	O	1
C support	½"	1"	4"	O	1
D headrest	½"	1¼"	4"	O	1
E backrest	⅜"	2¼"	5⅝"	O	1
F base	½"	8"	6"	O	2
G table top	½"	12" dia.		O	1

Material Key: O–oak
Supplies: 11—¼ X1" toy axle pegs, 3/16"dowel, ¼" dowel, ¼" hardboard, finish.

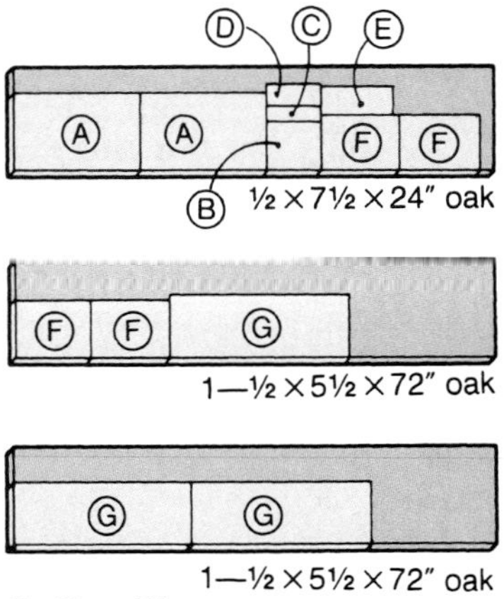
D
C
E
A
A
F
F
B
½ × 7½ × 24" oak
F
F
G
1—½ × 5½ × 72" oak
G
G
1—½ × 5½ × 72" oak

Cutting Diagram

Assemble the chair

1. Dry-assemble the chair to make certain parts fit. Apply glue (we used white woodworker's glue) to the holes in the seat, position it between the chair sides, and then insert the 1"-long toy axle pegs through the two holes in each side and into the holes in the seat.

2. Follow the same procedure to add the seat support and headrest. Clamp to squeeze the chair assembly together. (We used bar clamps.) Wipe off any glue squeeze-out. Glue the 3/16" dowel in the headrest, position the backrest, and glue the horizontal toy axle peg in the bottom. Cut the shafts on two toy axle pegs to ¼" long. Glue them in the top holes of the headrest.

Turn to the table

1. For the table base, rip and crosscut two pieces (F) from ½" oak to 4¼ X13". (See the Table Assembly drawing *above*) Glue the edges making one 8½ X13" lamination. Crosscut the lamination in half to form two 6 7/16"-long pieces. Place double-faced tape on the face of one piece, and then stack the se-

continued

TEA-FOR-TWO DINING SET
continued

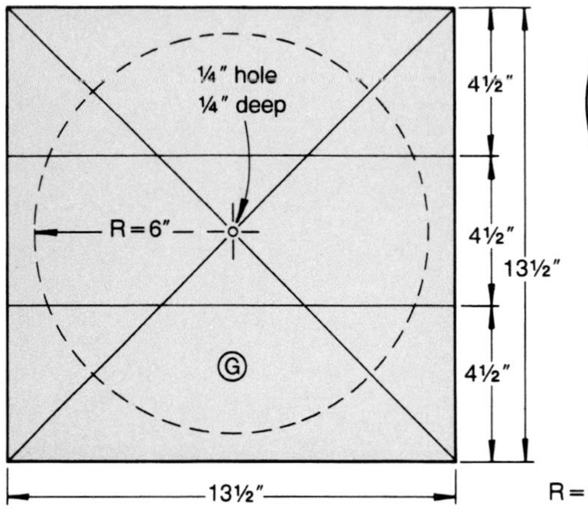

TABLETOP LAMINATION DRAWING

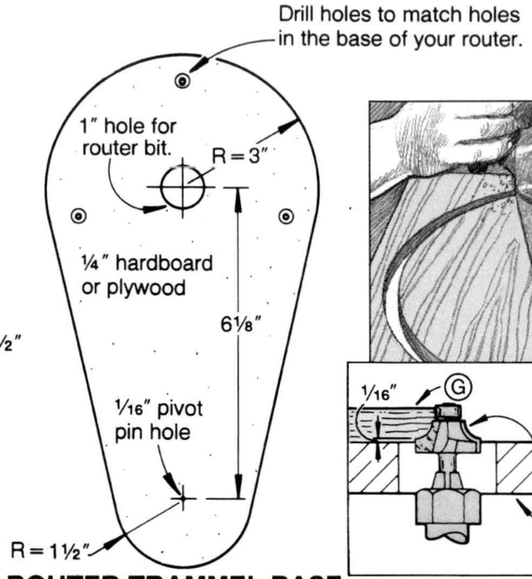

ROUTER TRAMMEL BASE

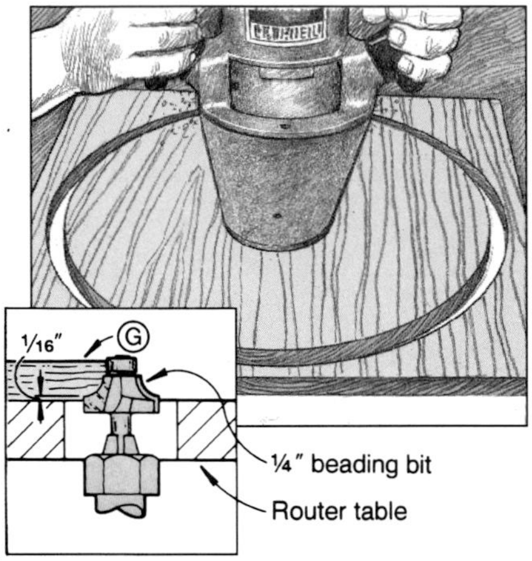

cond on top of it. Align the edges. Next, trace the full-sized Table Base half-pattern on the top piece. Flip the pattern over and trace the other half of the table base to make a complete pattern. Using a scrollsaw, saw the base parts to shape, cutting outside of the line, and then sanding to the line. (We used a drum sander on the drill press.) Separate the pieces, and remove the tape.

2. Lay out the 3"-long notches in the table base pieces. Cut one in the bottom-half of one piece (solid line on pattern), and one in the top-half (dotted line on pattern) of the other base piece. (We used a scrollsaw.) Finish-sand the two parts.

3. To make the tabletop (G), rip and crosscut three pieces of ½" oak to 4½ x13½". Glue-join the pieces edge to edge as shown in the Tabletop Lamination drawing *above*. Clamp (we used bar clamps). Once the glue dries, scrape off any squeeze-out, and sand.

4. Draw diagonal lines on the underside of the lamination to find the centerpoint. Drive a #4 finish nail part way through the lamination at the centerpoint. Clip off the head of the nail leaving about ¾" exposed. (The finish nail serves as the pivot point for the trammel.) Next, using ¼"-thick hardboard and the dimensions on the trammel drawing *above right,* make a trammel to fit your router. Now, mount the trammel to your router, and, using a ¼" straight bit, rout the disc to a 12" diameter as shown *above right*. (We increased the cutting depth in ¼" increments.) Remove the nail from the disc, and drill a ¼" hole ¼" deep at the centerpoint.

5. Mount your router to a router table, and chuck a ¼" beading bit in the collet. Now, rout a bead along the top edge of the table top as shown in the routing detail insert *above right*. (The surface with the ¼" hole in the center should be the underside of the tabletop.) Finish-sand the tabletop.

6. Using the dimensions on the Table Base pattern, mark and drill the ¼" dowel holes ¼" deep into the tops of the two base pieces. (We used a doweling jig.) Sand a slight round-over only on the edges of the base parts where indicated on the Exploded View drawing. Finally, assemble the base. Cut five ¼" dowels ½" long and glue them in the holes in the top of the base.

7. Turn the tabletop upside down (¼" hole up). Lay a straightedge across the center of the hole, lightly draw a line, and mark a centerpoint 2¼" on both sides of the center hole. Next, using a square, mark a second line perpendicular (90°) to the first, and mark centerpoints 2¼" from the center on both sides. Drill the four ¼" holes ¼" deep in the tabletop.

8. Test assemble the table for fit. Now, apply glue in the dowel holes, insert the dowels in the base into the holes in the top, and lightly tap until the top sets flush on the base.

9. Apply the finish of your choice. (We applied a light oil stain, and then three coats of polyurethane, sanding lightly between coats.)

Buying Guide

• **Oak stock.** Three pieces ½x7¼ x36", catalog no. 5LU274. For current prices, contact Constantine, 2050 Eastchester Rd., Bronx, NY 10461, or call 800-223-8087.

Project Tool List

Tablesaw
Scrollsaw
Router
  Router table
  Bits: ⅛" round-over, ¼" straight, ¼" beading
Drill
  Doweling jig
Drill press
  Sanding drum
  Bits: 1/16", 3/16" ¼", 1"
Finishing sander

Note: *We built the project using the tools listed. You may be able to substitute other tools or equipment for listed items you don't have. Additional common tools and clamps may be required to complete the project.*

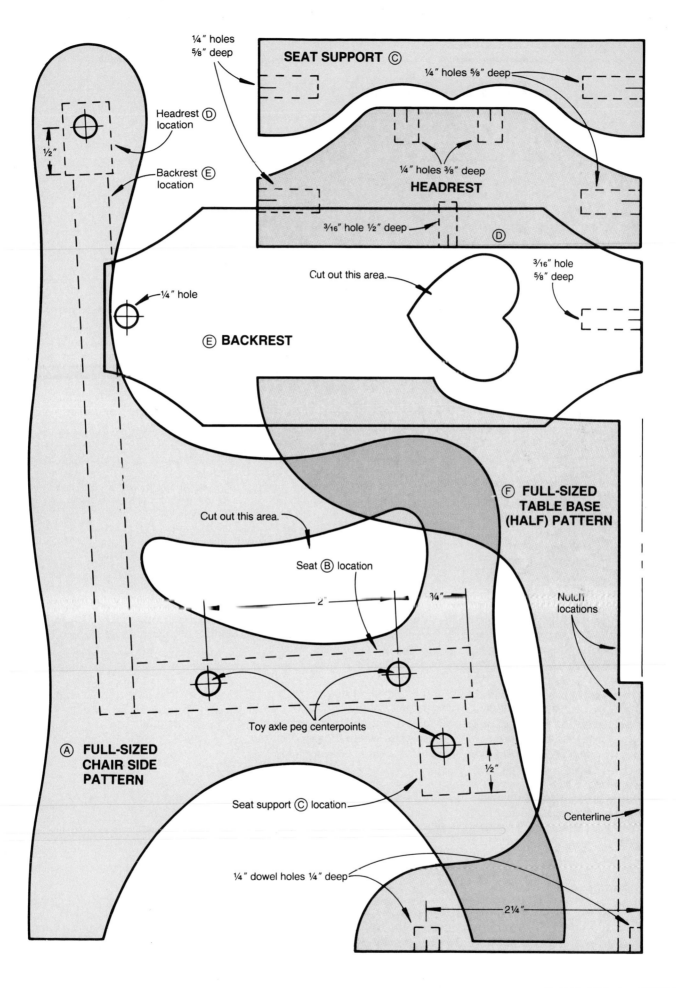

SEAT SUPPORT Ⓒ

¼" holes
⅝" deep

¼" holes ⅝" deep

¼" holes ⅜" deep

HEADREST

³⁄₁₆" hole ½" deep

Ⓓ

Headrest Ⓓ
location

Backrest Ⓔ
location

½"

¼" hole

Ⓔ **BACKREST**

Cut out this area.

³⁄₁₆" hole
⅝" deep

Ⓕ **FULL-SIZED
TABLE BASE
(HALF) PATTERN**

Cut out this area.

Seat Ⓑ location

2"

¾"

Notch
locations

Toy axle peg centerpoints

Ⓐ **FULL-SIZED
CHAIR SIDE
PATTERN**

½"

Seat support Ⓒ location

Centerline

¼" dowel holes ¼" deep

2¼"

KING ARTHUR'S CASTLE

When assembled, it's hard to tell our castle from the real McCoy. Made from maple turning squares, plywood, and boards, this project will delight collectors and young historians alike. You can buy the plastic Britain knights at local hobby shops, or order from our Buying Guide source on *page 89.*

Start with the towers

1. Square three rough 3x3x36" maple turning squares. (See the Buying Guide for a mail order source. Or, laminate ¾" stock to make up the 3x3" and 2x2" parts.) To square them, plane two adjacent sides, set your tablesaw's rip

fence 3" from the blade, and then rip the two opposite sides.

2. To make the corner towers (A), crosscut four 15" lengths from two of the squares. For the gate towers (B), crosscut one 16" length from the third square. Draw diagonal lines to find the centerpoint on the top end of the 15"-long tower pieces and on both ends of the 16"-long gate tower piece.

3. Using your tablesaw and an auxiliary rip fence, bevel-rip the four corners (making eight sides) on each square to the dimensions shown on the Bevel/Notch Detail on the Tower Drawing *opposite.* (We set the rip fence 2⅛" from the

sawblade, lowered it to ½", tilted it 45°, and made the cuts.)

4. Chuck a 2"-diameter Forstner-type bit in your drill press. Bore a hole 1¾" deep in the top of a corner tower as shown *below.* Bore

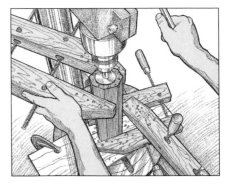

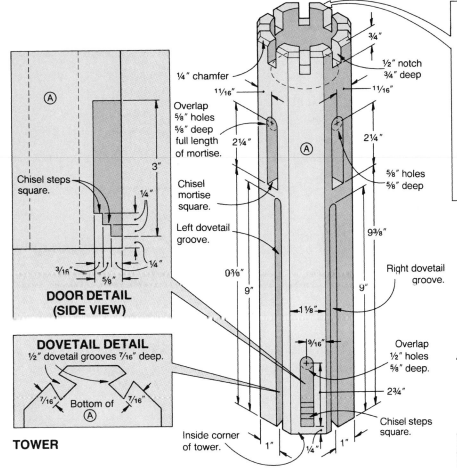

DOOR DETAIL (SIDE VIEW)

¼" chamfer

A

Chisel steps square.

3"

¼"

3/16"

5/8"

¼"

DOVETAIL DETAIL

½" dovetail grooves 7/16" deep.

7/16"

Bottom of A

7/16"

TOWER

Overlap 5/8" holes 5/8" deep full length of mortise.

11/16"

2¼"

A

Chisel mortise square.

Left dovetail groove.

9⅜"

0¾0"

9"

1⅛"

9/16"

Inside corner of tower.

1"

¼"

1"

¾"

½" notch ¾" deep

11/16"

2¼"

5/8" holes 5/8" deep

9⅜"

9"

Right dovetail groove.

Overlap ½" holes 5/8" deep.

2¾"

Chisel steps square.

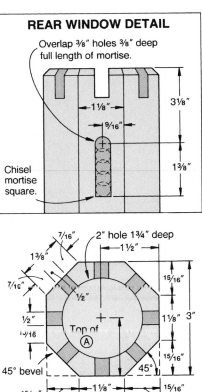

REAR WINDOW DETAIL

Overlap 3/8" holes 3/8" deep full length of mortise.

1⅛"

9/16"

Chisel mortise square.

3⅛"

1⅜"

BEVEL/NOTCH DETAIL

7/16"

2" hole 1¾" deep

1½"

1⅜"

7/16"

½"

½"

1/16"

Top of A

15/16"

1⅛" 3"

15/16"

45° bevel

15/16"

1⅛"

15/16"

3"

45°

---

the other tower pieces, and both ends of the 16" length. Bore slowly and remove the bit from the work frequently to avoid overheating it.

5. Lay out the door or passageway and three window locations on each corner tower where dimensioned on the Tower drawing and on the Rear Window detail. To form the side windows, bore overlapping ⅝"-diameter holes ⅝" deep. (We used a Forstner bit.) Drill overlapping ½"-diameter holes ⅝" deep to form the passageway. (See the Door detail *above.*) When boring the passageway, make the bottom shallower so you can chisel in the stair steps. Drill ⅜"-diameter overlapping holes ⅜" deep for the rear window in each corner tower. Chisel the bottom of all windows square. Chisel two steps in each passageway.

6. Mark the centerlines for the left and right dovetail slots on each corner tower. (See Dovetail detail *above.*) Chuck a ½" dovetail bit into

your table-mounted router and elevate it 7/16" above the table, and lock in place. Test setting on scrap

7. To cut the *left* dovetail grooves, position the fence 1¼" from the center of the bit. Clamp a stop block 9" (from bit center) ahead of the bit. Place a corner tower on the router table with the right dovetail side against the fence, the *left* dovetail side on the table surface, and the bottom of the tower against the bit. Next, rout the groove, pushing the tower forward until it touches your stop block. Stop the router and back the tower off the bit. Now, rout the left dovetail groove in the other corner towers the same way.

8. To rout the *right* dovetail groove, position the fence 1¾" from the center of the bit. Leave the stop block at 9". Place a corner tower on the router table with the *right* dovetail side on the table surface. Rout the groove, pushing the tower

continued

Bill of Materials					
Part		**Finished Size***		Mat.	Qty.
		T	W	L	
A	tower	3"	3"	15"	MT	4
D	tower	3"	3"	7⅜"	MT	2
C1	wall	¾"	31"	9"	MP	2
C2	wall	¾"	24"	9"	MP	2
D	gate liner	¼"	1⅜"	4⅞"	M	2
E	gate guide	¾"	1½"	8⅝"	M	2
F1*	plinth	½"	⅝"	10³/₁₆"	M	2
F2**	plinth	½"	⅝"	23¼"	M	2
F3**	plinth	½"	⅝"	30¼"	M	1
G1	battlement	2"	2"	30¼"	M	2
G2	battlement	2"	2"	23¼"	M	2
H	battlement	2"	2"	4"	M	1
I	gate	¼"	3⅜"	5½"	M	1
J	latch	¼"	¼"	⅞"	M	1
K	draw bridge	¼"	3⅞"	5⅛"	M	1

*Cut part marked with * to fit front wall. Cut length of part marked with ** to fit side walls. Cut length of part marked with *** to fit rear wall.

Material Key: MT—maple turning squares; MP—maple plywood, M—maple
Supplies: #18X⅝" brads, paint, finish.

KING ARTHUR'S CASTLE
continued

forward until it touches the stop block. Stop the router and remove the tower. Rout the right dovetail groove in the other corner towers.

9. To cut the crenellated tower tops, mount a ½"-wide dado on your tablesaw and elevate it to cut ¾" deep. Next, attach an auxiliary fence to your saw's miter gauge so it extends at least 4" beyond the dado blade. Using the dimensions on the Bevel/Notch detail *(page 85)*, mark the location of each ½"-wide groove on the sides at the top of each tower, and both top and bottom of the 16" length.

10. Place one of the towers top-down on the saw table and against the auxiliary fence. Align your marks with the dado blade, and cut a groove through the top. Remove the tower, return the miter gauge/auxiliary fence to the front of the table, rotate the tower one-eighth turn to expose the next side, align the marks with the blade, and cut a groove. Rotate the tower two more times to cut the remaining grooves. Now, dado the other corner towers and both ends of the 16"-long gate tower piece.

11. Remount your saw blade and angle it at 45°. Now, cut the ¼"-wide chamfer on the tops of the four corner towers and both ends of the gate tower piece. Sand all surfaces and edges on the pieces.

GATE TOWER DRAWINGS

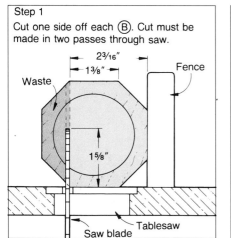

Step 1
Cut one side off each Ⓑ. Cut must be made in two passes through saw.

2³/₁₆"
1⅜"
Waste
Fence
1⅝"
Tablesaw
Saw blade

12. To finish forming the gate towers (B), set up your tablesaw as shown in Step 1 of the Gate Tower drawings *below left*. Rip the 16"-long tower piece. Next, cross-cut the piece 7⅞" from each end. Saw a notch out of the inside corner on both where shown in the Step 2 drawing *below*, and as shown *above*.

Make the walls next

1. From ¾" maple plywood, and using the dimensions in the Bill of Materials, rip and crosscut two long (C1) and two short (C2) wall sections. Note grain direction of the plywood on the Cutting Diagram on *page 89*.

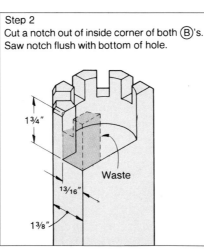

Step 2
Cut a notch out of inside corner of both Ⓑ's. Saw notch flush with bottom of hole.

1¾"
Waste
1³/₁₆"
1⅜"

2. Set up your table-mounted router with the dovetail bit and a fence to make the cuts shown in the Dovetail detail on the Front-Wall drawing *opposite*. (Two cuts are required.) Test-cut a dovetail tenon along the end of a scrap piece of ¾" plywood to make sure the tenon fits the tower dovetail slots. Dovetail both ends on each wall section.

3. Lay out and cut the gate opening on the face of one long wall section where dimensioned on the Front-Wall drawing. This will be the castle's front wall.

4. To prepare ¼"-thick stock for pieces D, I, J, and K, first crosscut a ¾"-thick 5½"-wide piece of maple to 12" long. Plane it to ¼" thickness. Rip a 1⅜"-wide strip from one edge for the gate liners (D). (See the Cutting Diagram.) Set the remaining piece aside.

5. Saw a ⅛" chamfer along one edge of the 1⅜"-wide piece. Cross-cut it into two 4⅞"-long pieces for the liners (D). Glue (we used yellow woodworker's glue), and clamp the liners in the gate opening where shown on the Bottom View Section.

6. To make the gate guides (E), rip and crosscut a piece of ¾" maple to 1½ X 18". Cut a ¼" rabbet ⅛" deep along one edge of the piece. Cut a ⁵/₁₆" wide, ¼"-deep groove on the same face, ⅜" in from the opposite edge (see the Front Wall drawing). Next, crosscut the piece to form two 8⅜"-long pieces. Using double-faced tape, tape the two pieces inside face to inside face and then cut the ¼"-wide, ⅛"-deep notch.

7. Scribe a ¾" radius on the top end of the gate guides. Cut the radius on a bandsaw or scrollsaw, and then sand. Separate the pieces, remove the tape, and glue them to the inside of the front wall where shown on the Bottom View Section.

8. To make the castle wall plinths (F1,F2,F3), bevel-rip a ¼" chamfer on one 36" length and three 24"

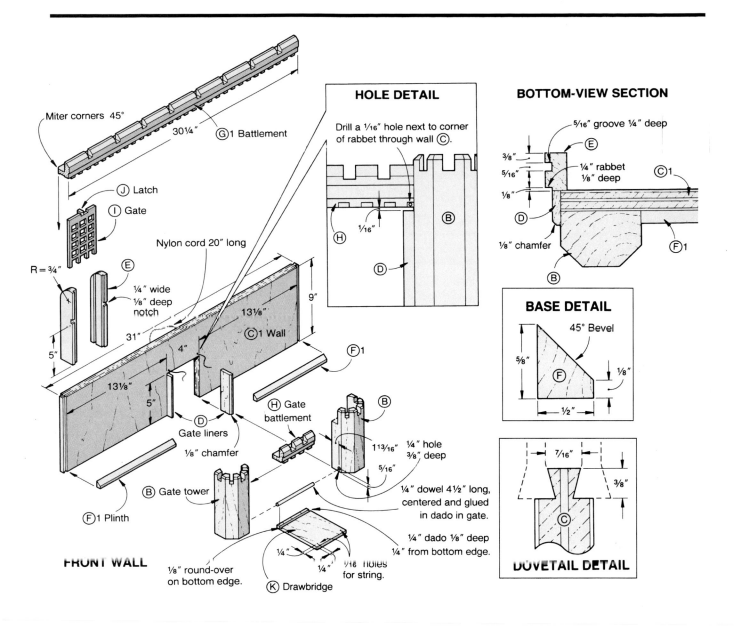

HOLE DETAIL

Drill a ¹⁄₁₆″ hole next to corner of rabbet through wall C.

BOTTOM-VIEW SECTION

⁵⁄₁₆″ groove ¼″ deep

E

³⁄₈″

¼″ rabbet ⅛″ deep

⁵⁄₁₆″

C1

⅛″

D

⅛″ chamfer

B

F1

BASE DETAIL

45° Bevel

⅝″

F

⅛″

½″

DUVETAIL DETAIL

⁷⁄₁₆″

³⁄₈″

C

Miter corners 45°

30¼″ G1 Battlement

J Latch

I Gate

R = ¾″

Nylon cord 20″ long

E

¼″ wide ⅛″ deep notch

31″

4″

13⅛″

C1 Wall

9″

5″

13⅛″

5″

D

Gate liners

⅛″ chamfer

F1 Plinth

B Gate tower

H Gate battlement

B

1¹³⁄₁₆″

⁵⁄₁₆″

¼″ hole ³⁄₈″ deep

¼″ dowel 4½″ long, centered and glued in dado in gate.

¼″ dado ⅛″ deep ¼″ from bottom edge.

⅛″ round-over on bottom edge.

¼″

¼″

¹⁄₁₆″ holes for string.

K Drawbridge

FRONT WALL

lengths of ¾″ maple stock. Next, rip the pieces to ½″ wide. Crosscut the lengths to fit along the bottom of each wall section. Glue and clamp these pieces along the base of the appropriate wall sections.

Now, make the battlements

1. To make the front and rear wall battlements (G1), the side wall battlements (G2), and the gate battlement (H), square two 36″-long and two 24″-long turning squares to 2×2″. Crosscut the longest squares (G) to 30¼″. Crosscut the two 24″ squares to 23¼″ long for the side wall. Make the gate battlement from one of the cutoff pieces. Refer to the dimensions on the

Battlement drawing on *page 88* and lay out the location of the dadoes on one long piece. Use dimensions on the Gate Battlement detail to lay out the cuts on that piece.

Note: *With the exception of cutting the ¾″-wide groove in the bottom face of the wall battlements (Step 1), the gate battlement requires the same shaping steps (2 through 7). To save time, work the gate battlement after you've worked the wall battlement at each step, before changing your equipment for the next step.*

2. Mount a ¾″-wide dado blade to your tablesaw. Dado a groove in a piece of scrap and test the groove's fit on the edge of a wall section. Adjust for a snug fit. Now, as directed

by Step 1 on the same drawing, rip the ¾″-wide groove ⅜″ deep in the bottom face of each square.

3. Adjust the dado head to make a ½″-wide cut. Using the miter gauge, crosscut the ½″-wide ⅝″-deep dadoes every 3″ along the top face of each wall battlement piece where shown in Step 2. A radial saw will be more convenient for making these cuts. (We set stop blocks and the fence when making the crosscuts.) Crosscut the ½″-wide dadoes in the top of the gate battlement.

4. Crosscut the ½″-wide dadoes ¼″ deep and ½″ apart along the bottom of each battlement (Step 3).
continued

KING ARTHUR'S CASTLE

continued

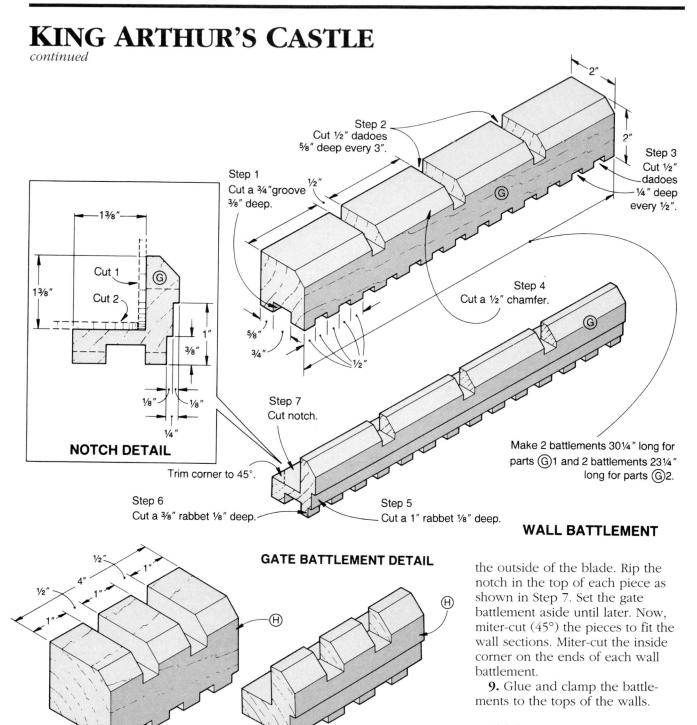

NOTCH DETAIL

Step 1
Cut a ¾" groove
⅜" deep.

Step 2
Cut ½" dadoes
⅝" deep every 3".

Step 3
Cut ½" dadoes
¼" deep every ½".

Step 4
Cut a ½" chamfer.

Step 5
Cut a 1" rabbet ⅛" deep.

Step 6
Cut a ⅜" rabbet ⅛" deep.

Step 7
Cut notch.

Trim corner to 45°.

Make 2 battlements 30¼" long for parts Ⓖ1 and 2 battlements 23¼" long for parts Ⓖ2.

WALL BATTLEMENT

GATE BATTLEMENT DETAIL

Cut molding same as Ⓖ except note locations and dimensions of dado. There is no groove in bottom.

the outside of the blade. Rip the notch in the top of each piece as shown in Step 7. Set the gate battlement aside until later. Now, miter-cut (45°) the pieces to fit the wall sections. Miter-cut the inside corner on the ends of each wall battlement.

9. Glue and clamp the battlements to the tops of the walls.

Build that gate and drawbridge

1. From the remaining ¼"-thick stock, rip and crosscut a 3⅜×5½" piece. Use the dimensions on the Gate Drawing *opposite* to lay out the grid for the gate (I). Drill ¼"-start holes in each rectangle. Scroll-saw the 15 rectangles in the gate. Next, sand the 45° bevel along the top of the gate. Now, scrollsaw a notch in the top for the latch.

5. Mount your regular saw blade and angle it to 45° from vertical. As explained in Step 4, rip the ½" chamfer along the top front edge on all battlement pieces.

6. Return the saw blade to vertical, elevate it to 1" above the

table. Cut the ⅛"-wide rabbet along the bottom front edge (Step 5).

7. Lower the saw blade to ⅜". Rip the ⅛"-wide rabbet along the bottom edge of each piece (Step 6).

8. Elevate the saw blade to 1⅜", set your saw's rip fence 1⅜" from

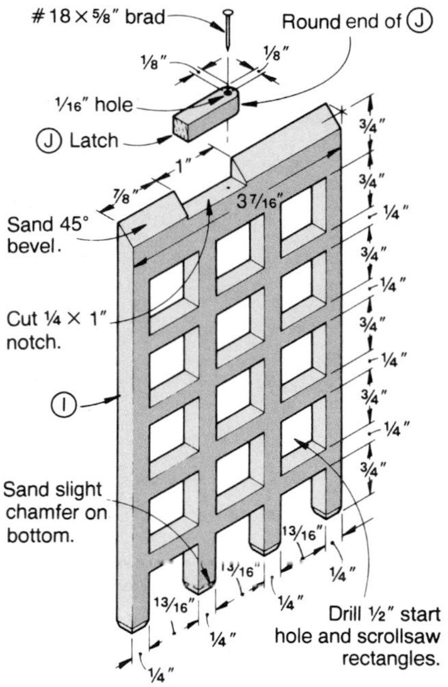

#18 × ⅝" brad
Round end of J
⅛"
⅛"
1⁄16" hole
J Latch
1"
⅞"
Sand 45° bevel.
3 7⁄16"
Cut ¼ × 1" notch.
I
Sand slight chamfer on bottom.
¾"
¼"
13⁄16"
Drill ½" start hole and scrollsaw rectangles.

GATE

CUTTING DIAGRAM

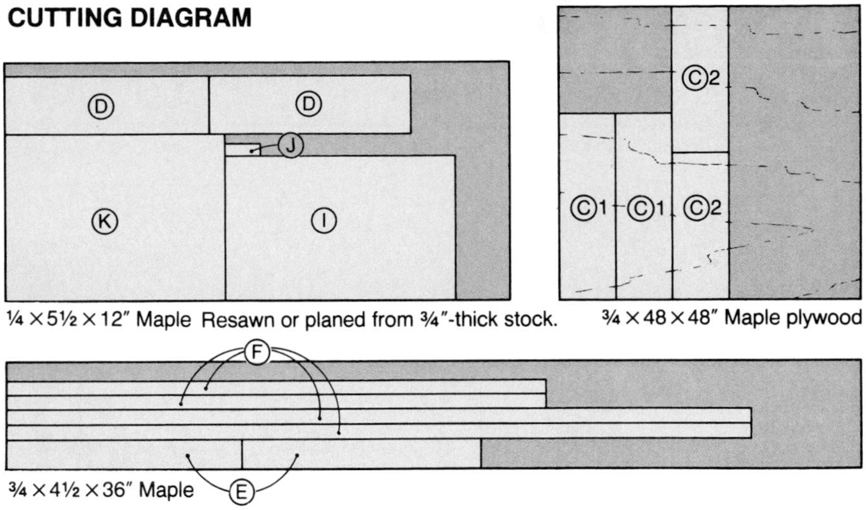

D
D
J
K
I
¼ × 5½ × 12" Maple Resawn or planed from ¾"-thick stock.
C2
C1
C1
C2
¾ × 48 × 48" Maple plywood
F
¾ × 4½ × 36" Maple
E

2. Saw the ¼x¼x⅞" latch (J) from scrap. Drill a 1⁄16" hole in it where shown on the Gate drawing, sand the corners round, and then nail it in the gate notch. Leave the latch loose enough to turn.

3. To make the drawbridge (K), rip and crosscut a 3⅞x5⅛" piece from the remaining ¼"-thick stock. Crosscut the ¼" dado ⅛" deep starting ¼" up from the bottom on the inside. Mark the two 1⁄16" string holes at the top of the drawbridge and drill them. Sand a ⅛" round-over along the bottom outside edge of the drawbridge. (We sanded the edge on our belt sander.) Using a straightedge and knife, cut shallow striations lengthwise and about ⅜" apart on both faces of the drawbridge to resemble planks. Crosscut a 4½"-long length of ¼" dowel and sand the ends so they'll turn freely in a ¼"-diameter hole. Now, center, glue, and clamp the dowel in the drawbridge groove.

4. Using dimensions on the Front Wall drawing, mark the centerpoints for the ¼" holes for the drawbridge dowel on the inside faces of the two gate towers. Drill the holes ⅜" deep. Next, using dimensions on the Hole detail on the same drawing, locate and drill two 1⁄16" holes for the drawbridge string. Thread the ends of a 20"-long nylon cord (we used builder's line) through the holes from the back.

5. Glue and clamp a gate tower to the front wall (see the Bottom View Section). Place the drawbridge's dowel in the hole at the base of that tower. Next, apply glue to the other gate tower, and then insert the dowel in its ¼"-diameter hole as you position the tower on the front wall. Clamp both gate towers until the glue dries. Thread the ends of your cord through the holes in the top of the drawbridge. Tie a knot in one end, adjust the cord so the bridge sits where you want it, tie off the other end, and cut off the excess.

6. Crosscut the gate battlement to fit between the gate towers. Lay the wall down with the gate towers on top and glue on the battlement.

Go, and hold down the fort

1. Finish-sand all parts. Wipe or blow away the sanding dust. Paint the interiors of the tower tops, windows, and doors (we used a slat gray color). Apply the finish of your choice. (We decided to leave the maple natural and applied two coats of spray lacquer.) Sand with 320-grit sandpaper after each coat.

2. To assemble the castle, slide the dovetail tongue on the ends of each wall section into the dovetail grooves in the corner towers.

Buying Guide

- **Maple turning squares.** Package of three 3x3x36", two 2x2x36", and two 2x2x24" squares. Rough on two sides. Catalog no. WD 1990. For current prices, contact Constantine, 2050 Eastchester Rd., Bronx, NY 10461-2297, or call 800-223-8087.
- **Toy soldiers.** Type pictured are painted (unpainted available) hard plastic on metal base. For current prices, contact Castle Soldiers, The Toy Soldier Co., 100 Riverside Dr., New York, NY 10024, or call 212-799-6348.

Project Tool List

Tablesaw
  Dado blade or dado set
Scrollsaw
Planer
Belt sander
Router
  Router table
  ½" dovetail bit
Drill press
  Bits: 1⁄16", ¼", ⅜", ½", ⅝", 2"
Finishing sander

Note: *We built the project using the tools listed. You may be able to substitute other tools or equipment for listed items you don't have. Additional common tools and clamps may be required to complete the project.*

FASHION-DOLL ARMOIRE

Children never forget those very special gifts you make for them. Our cherry fashion-doll armoire, sized to match popular dolls such as Mattel's Barbie®, stands as the perfect example.

Note: *Besides the ¾" stock, you'll also need ½"- and ¼"-thick material for several parts. If you can't buy*

thin stock locally, plane or resaw thicker material to these thicknesses.

Start with the curved top and the bottom

1. To form the top (A), rip and crosscut two ¾"-thick pieces to 5½x8". (We used cherry.) See the Cutting Diagram *opposite*. Glue and clamp the two pieces face to face, aligning all edges. (We used yellow woodworker's glue.) After the glue

dries, remove the clamps and trim the lamination to the final dimensions of 5⅛x7⅞".

2. From ¾" cherry stock, rip and crosscut a piece to 5x7⅞" for the armoire's bottom (B).

3. Rout an ¹¹⁄₁₆" rabbet ¼" deep along the front and side edges of the top, and along the sides of the bottom as detailed on the Exploded View drawing *opposite*, and

continued

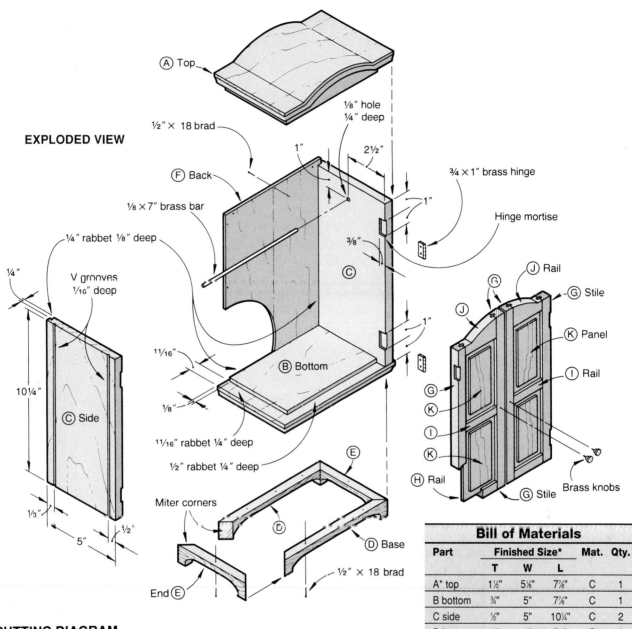

EXPLODED VIEW

(A) Top

½″ × 18 brad

(F) Back

⅛ × 7″ brass bar

¼″ rabbet ⅛″ deep

V grooves 1/16″ deep

¼″

10¼″

(C) Side

⅓″

5″

½″

1″

2½″

⅛″ hole ¼″ deep

¾ × 1″ brass hinge

Hinge mortise

1″

3/8″

(C)

1″

11/16″

(B) Bottom

⅛″

11/16″ rabbet ¼″ deep

½″ rabbet ¼″ deep

Miter corners

(D)

End (E)

(E)

(D) Base

½″ × 18 brad

(G)

(J) Rail

(G) Stile

(J)

(K) Panel

(J)

(I) Rail

(G)

(K)

(I)

(K)

(H) Rail

(G) Stile

Brass knobs

	Bill of Materials			
Part	**Finished Size***		**Mat.**	**Qty.**
	T	**W**	**L**		
A* top	1½″	5⅛″	7⅞″	C	1
B bottom	¾″	5″	7⅞″	C	1
C side	½″	5″	10¼″	C	2
D base	½″	1″	7½″	C	2
E base	½″	1″	4¾″	C	2
F back	⅛″	7 1/16″	10¼″	P	1
G stile	½″	½″	10⅞″	C	4
H rail	½″	½″	2 3/16″	C	2
I rail	½″	½″	2 3/16″	C	2
J rail	½″	1¼″	2 3/16″	C	2
K panel	¼″	2½″	4⅝″	C	4

*Part marked with * laminated from two ¾″-thick pieces.

Material Key: C—cherry, P—cherry plywood
Supplies: ⅛″ brass rod, ⅜″ brass cup hooks, ¾×1″ or smaller brass hinges, 4d finish nails, #18×½″ brads, 2—7/16″-diameter brass screw knobs, finish.

CUTTING DIAGRAM

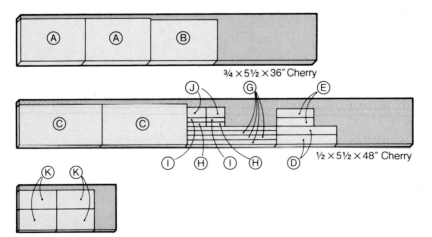

(A) (A) (B)

¾ × 5½ × 36″ Cherry

(C) (C)

(J) (G) (E)

(I) (H) (I) (H) (D)

½ × 5½ × 48″ Cherry

(K) (K)

¼ × 5½ × 12″ Cherry

FASHION-DOLL ARMOIRE

continued

also on the Top and Bottom Side View drawings *below*. Next, cut a ½" rabbet ¼" deep along the front edge of the bottom.

4. To accommodate the back panel, cut a ¼"-wide rabbet ⅛" deep along the back edge of both the top and bottom pieces where shown on the Exploded View drawing.

5. Make a paper copy of the Lower Curve pattern found on *page 95*. Next, make the routing template by cutting a ¾" piece of scrap to 7⅞x10". Adhere the paper pattern to one end of the piece, with the opening to the arch facing out.

Now, bandsaw the arch of the template to shape. Smooth the curve of the arch with a drum sander.

6. Clamp the top lamination in a bench vise (front facing up). Tack the template you just made to it, aligning the sides and front edge. (We placed the nails in areas of the top that will be cut away later.)

7. Attach a ¾" O.D. guide bushing to your router's base plate and chuck in a ½" straight bit. Place the router's base on top of the template. Using the template as a guide, rout the arch in the front edge of the top to match the ¾" rabbet depth as shown on the middle illustration *below left*. (The routed area measures about 4" long and ½" wide. We made this cut in ¼" increments to reach final depth.)

8. Elevate your saw blade to 1⅜" above the table. Position the rip fence ¾" from the inside face of the saw blade, place the top piece on edge with its *top face* against the fence, and then saw a kerf along that edge. Turn the top end for end and saw a kerf along that edge.

9. Remove the guide bushing from the router's base plate. Switch to a ⅝" high piloted cove bit, and set it to cut ⅛" deep. Next, rout along the lower edge on the front and both sides of your top piece, and the lower edge on the front and sides of the bottom. (When routing, we clamped a piece of scrap flush with the back edges to help stabilize the router.)

10. Make a paper pattern of the top's crown profile using the Top

TOP (SIDE VIEW)

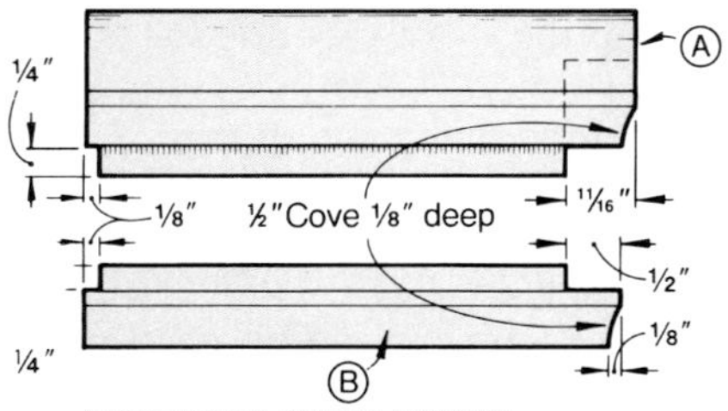

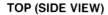

A
¼"
⅛"
½" Cove ⅛" deep
1/16"
½"
⅛"
¼"
B

BOTTOM (SIDE VIEW)

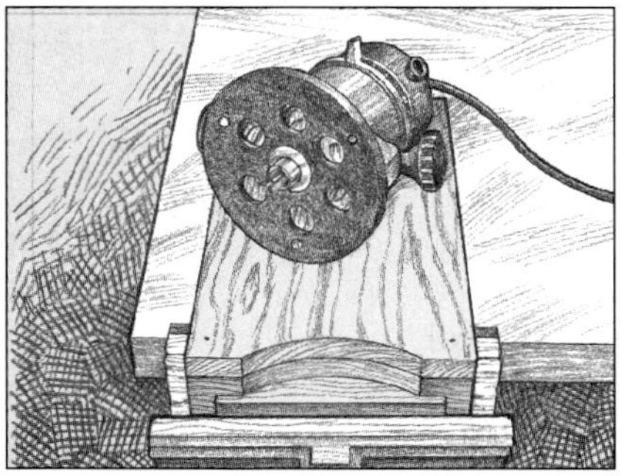

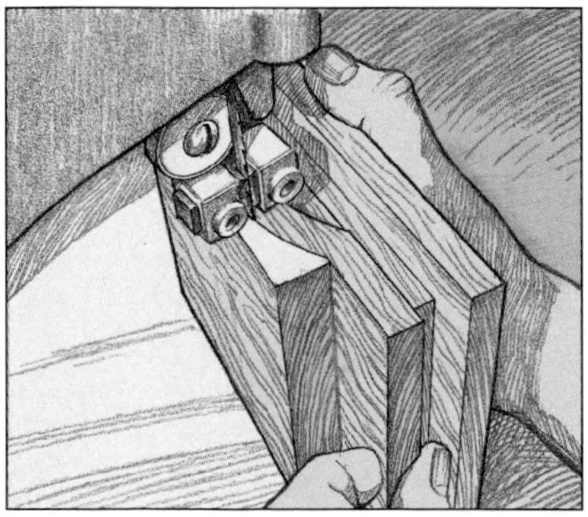

DOOR

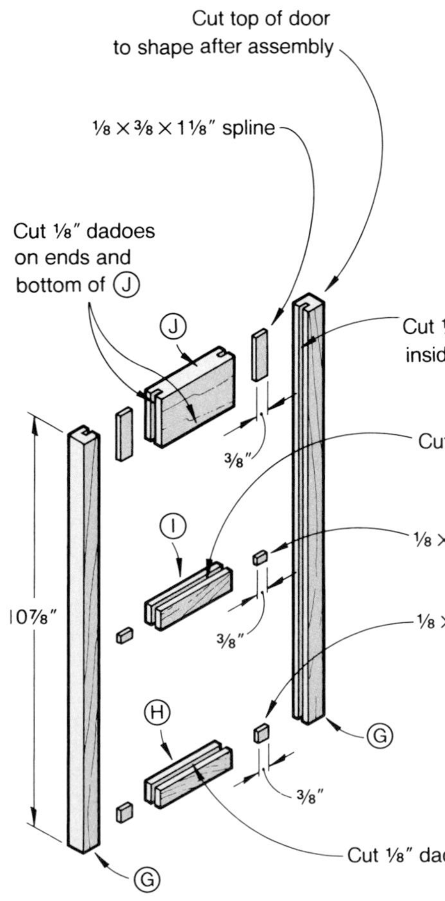

Cut top of door
to shape after assembly
⅛ x ⅜ x 1⅛" spline
Cut ⅛" dadoes
on ends and
bottom of J
J
Cut ⅛" dado on
inside edge of G
⅜"
Cut ⅛" dadoes on all edge of I
I
⅛ x ⅜ x ¼" spline
10⅞"
⅜"
⅛ x ⅜ x ⅜" spline
Note: Panels in door
not shown for clarity.
H
G
⅜"
G
Cut ⅛" dadoes on ends and top of H

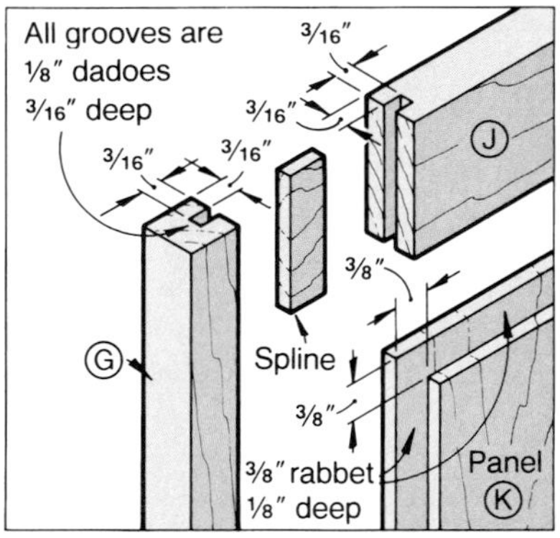

All grooves are
⅛" dadoes
3/16" deep
3/16"
3/16"
3/16"
3/16"
J
⅜"
G
Spline
⅜"
⅜" rabbet
⅛" deep
Panel
K

JOINT DETAIL

TOP DETAIL

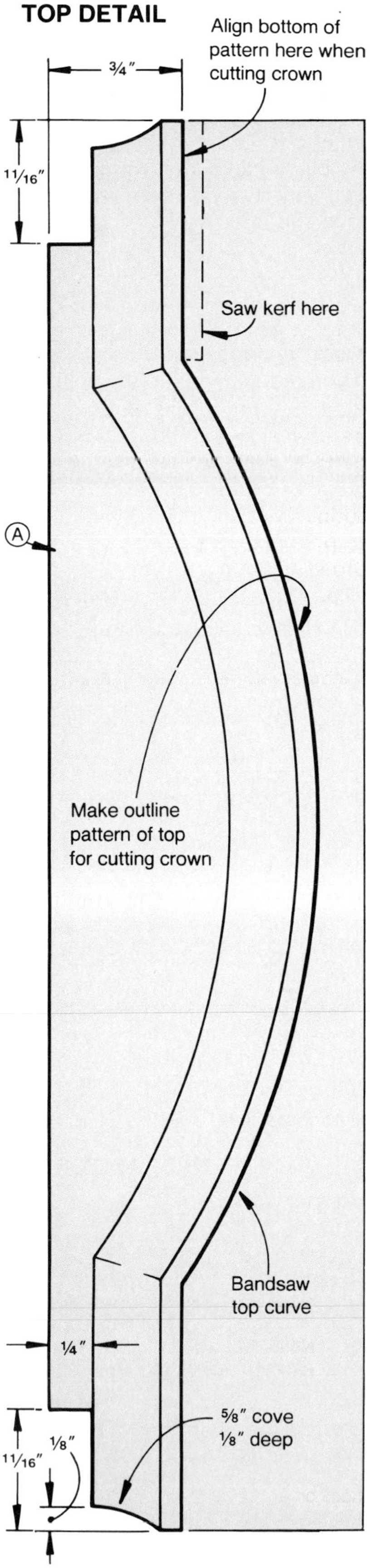

Align bottom of pattern here when cutting crown
3/4"
1 1/16"
Saw kerf here
A
Make outline pattern of top for cutting crown
Bandsaw top curve
1/4"
5/8" cove
1/8" deep
1/8"
1 1/16"

detail drawing *left*. Adhere it to the front edge of the top, aligning it where instructed on the pattern.

11. Next, bandsaw from the top surface to the saw kerfs to remove the block of waste wood on both ends. Now, starting at the top of the crown, carefully bandsaw toward the kerf as shown *opposite bottom,* to form one-half of the top's crown. (Note we taped a piece of scrap wood to our top to give it a more stable base for sawing.) Saw the other half the same way. Finish-sand the cut. (We wrapped sandpaper around a foam sanding block.)

Now, make the sides, back, and base parts

1. Rip and crosscut two pieces of ½" cherry to 5x10¼" for the sides (C). From the same ½" stock, cut two 1x9" strips for the front and back base parts (D), and two 1x6" strips for the base ends (E).

2. Cut a ¼x⅛" rabbet for the back panel along the back inside edge of both side pieces. (We cut these rabbets on our tablesaw.)

3. Mount an edge guide to your router. Next, using the 60° tip on a ¼" veining bit, rout the 1/16"-deep grooves in the outside faces of the side panels where dimensioned on the Exploded View drawing. Now, drill the ⅛"-diameter holes ¼" deep where dimensioned on the inside faces of the sides for a clothes bar.

4. Position the door hinges on the front inside edges of the side panels where dimensioned. Score around the hinge leaves with an X-acto knife. Next, chisel the mortises into both sides equal to the thickness of the hinge leaves.

5. Miter-crosscut the base pieces (D, E) to the lengths (long point to long point) listed on the Bill of Materials on *page 91*. Tape (with double-faced tape) the matching parts together and align.

6. Next, make a copy of the two base patterns found on *page 95*. Adhere them to the face of the respective parts, centering between the ends. Bandsaw the parts to shape, and sand the cut edges. Now, separate the parts and remove the tape. Finish-sand the pieces.

7. Glue and clamp the four base pieces together. Square the corners. (We used rubber bands and spring clamps to hold the base pieces together while the glue cured.)

Next, assemble the carcase

1. Cut the 7"-long brass clothes bar to length. Dry-fit the side panels, top, and bottom together, inserting the clothes bar in the holes. See the Exploded View drawing for details. Next glue, assemble, and clamp the side panels to the bottom. Check the assembly for square. Adjust if necessary. Nail the sides with 4d finish nails. (We drilled 1/16" pilot holes 1" deep for the nails.)

2. For the back panel (F), rip and crosscut a piece of ⅛" material (we used cherry plywood) to fit the opening. Glue and nail it in place with #18x½" brads.

3. Glue and nail the assembled base to the carcase bottom.

Now, let's make the doors

Note: *Measure the cabinet opening. (Ours measured 6½x10 5/16".) If necessary, adjust the dimensions of the door parts (G, H, I, J, K).*

1. From ½"-thick cherry, rip and crosscut six ½x12" pieces and one 1¼x12" piece. (We cut all pieces this long for safety while performing the following steps.)

2. Rip a ⅛"-wide dado 3/16" deep and centered along one edge of five of the ½x½x12" pieces. (See the Door drawing and Joint detail *opposite* for additional information) On the sixth 12"-long piece, cut the ⅛"-wide dado along *both* edges. (In a cross section the part will look like the letter H). Rip a dado centered along one edge of the 1¼" wide piece also.

3. Raise the saw blade, and using your miter gauge and a spacer block clamped to the rip fence, crosscut four of the ½x½x12" strips to 10⅞" long for the stiles (G). From the fifth ½x½x12" piece crosscut two 2 3/16" lengths for the bottom rails (H). Crosscut two 2 3/16"-long center rails (I) from the H-shaped piece. Crosscut two 2 3/16" lengths for the door top rails

continued

FASHION-DOLL ARMOIRE
continued

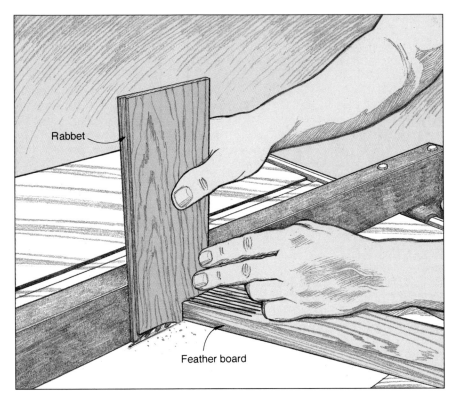

Rabbet

Feather board

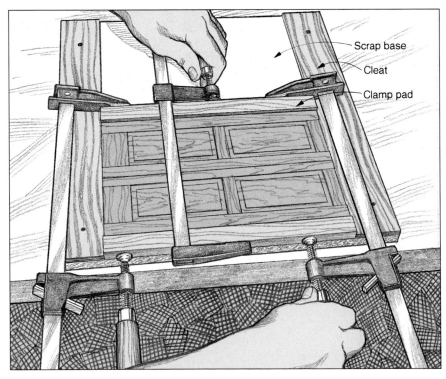

Scrap base

Cleat

Clamp pad

(J) from the 1¼x12" strip. (To help avoid confusion later, we lettered the parts as we cut them.)

4. Reset your saw's rip fence and blade to the settings used to cut the dadoes in step 2. (We used a previously cut door stile for resetting our saw and fence.) Cut a matching dado in the ends of all rail pieces.

5. Cut the four door panels (K) from ¼"-thick cherry to the dimensions listed on the Bill of Materials. To cut the panel rabbets, first attach an auxiliary wood fence to the rip fence, and then set it ⅛" from the inside edge of the blade.

6. Make a ⅛x6x20" auxiliary top (we used ⅛"-thick hardboard), place it on your tablesaw and against the fence, and clamp or tape it down. Next, elevate the saw blade through the auxiliary top until the blade measures ⅜" above the surface. Now, saw a kerf around all four edges of each door panel as shown *top left*.

7. To make the splines, rip and crosscut a 12" length of cherry stock to ⅛x⅜". Sand the strip to fit in the ⅛"-wide dadoes cut into the stiles and rails. Finish-sand all door parts. Test-assemble both doors, and cut the splines to length as you assemble the panels.

8. Glue, assemble, and square the doors. Next, center the panels within the frames, but do not glue them. Clamp the doors as shown at *left,* until the glue dries.

9. Make a copy of the Door Arch half pattern *opposite,* and cut it to shape. Tape the doors together back to back, aligning all edges. Position the pattern at the top, and trace its curve. Bandsaw both doors to shape. Now, separate the doors, remove the tape, and sand the edges.

10. Fit the doors into the carcass opening, allowing ¹⁄₁₆" clearance on all four sides. Sand the door edges if needed, to fit the opening.

FULL-SIZED PATTERNS

11. Screw the hinges to the side panels. Next, position the doors, and then mark the hinge location on them. Chisel the hinge mortises in the doors. Attach the doors to the hinges. Now, mark and drill pilot holes for the two door knobs.

Now, add the finishing touches

1. Finish-sand any areas needing touching up. Fill the visible nail holes with matching wood putty.

2. Trace the Hanger pattern at *right* onto a piece of ¼"-thick scrap. (We taped several layers together, and bandsawed them to shape at the same time.) Sand the hangers, and then screw a ⅜" brass cuphook into the center of each.

3. Apply the finish of your choice. (We left the cherry unstained, and sprayed on two light coats of water-based sealer. This we followed with three coats of a glossy water-based lacquer. We rubbed the finish lightly with a fine-textured Scotch-brite pad after each coat to level its surface.

4. Finally, attach the door knobs.

BARBIE trademark and ©1993 by Mattel, Inc. Used with permission. BARBIE® doll shown for illustration only. This armoire plan is not connected with Mattel, Inc.

Project Tool List
Tablesaw
Bandsaw
Drill press
　Sanding drum
　Bits: ¹⁄₁₆", ⅛"
Router
　¾" guide bushing
　Bits: ¼" veining, ½" straight,
　　½" cove
Finishing sander

Note: *We built the project using the tools listed. You may be able to substitute other tools or equipment for listed items you don't have. Additional common tools and clamps may be required to complete the project.*

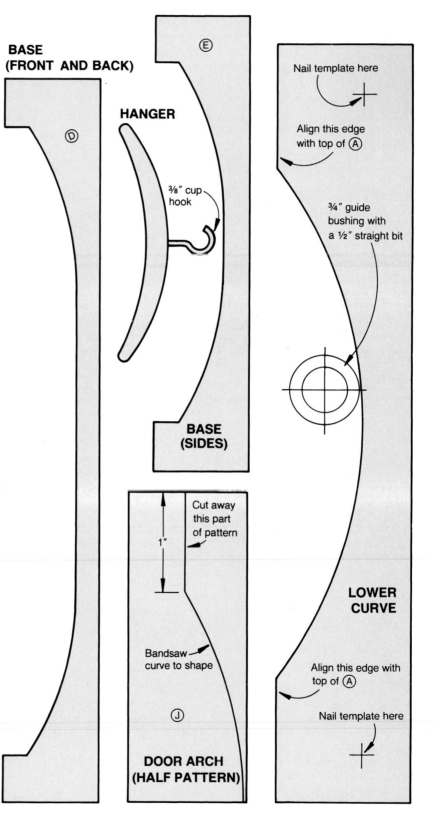

BASE (FRONT AND BACK)

HANGER

⅜" cup hook

BASE (SIDES)

E

D

Nail template here

Align this edge with top of (A)

¾" guide bushing with a ½" straight bit

LOWER CURVE

Align this edge with top of (A)

Nail template here

Cut away this part of pattern

1"

Bandsaw curve to shape

J

DOOR ARCH (HALF PATTERN)

ACKNOWLEDGMENTS

Project Designers

Arthur Anderson—Udderly Funny Rocking Cow, pages 22–25

Harry Billings—Patty Apatosaurus, pages 18–21

James Boelling—King Arthur's Castle, pages 84–89

Steven Bruni—The Heavy Haulin' Loader, pages 33–35

James R. Downing—Rough 'N' Ready Wrecker, pages 36–39; Noah's Lovable Ark, pages 67–68; Milk Truck & Pickup, pages 69–71; Tea-For-Two Dining Set, pages 80–83

Clint Hansen—Rubber-Band Dragster, pages 40–43

Harlequin Crafts—Noah's Lovable Ark, pages 67–68

Jeff Hayes—Barbie®'s Dreamworld, pages 76–79; Fashion-Doll Armoire, pages 90–95

Richard Jennum—Li'l Sod Buster Toy Tractor, pages 60–63

Bill Kaiser—Tiny Tyke Toolbox 'N' Tools, pages 72–75

Earl Lambert—Puzzled Pussycat, pages 5–7

David Lanford—Sea Skipper for Young Fliers, pages 64–65

Tom Lewis Wooden Toys—Red-Hot Fire Truck, pages 44–47; Whirlybird on a String, pages 56–59

Richard Milam—Rock 'N' Roll Wiggle Worm, pages 14–17

Greg Rounds—Giddyap Rocking Horse, pages 26–29

Harold Rupert Jr.—The Learning Train, pages 48–52

Hank Smith—Hop-Along Grasshopper, pages 10–13

Wood 'N' Art—King of the Caterpillars, pages 8–9

Darryl Yeager—One Honey of a Bee, pages 30–31

Jim Zeller—The U.S.S. Wood Funtime Fleet, pages 53–55

Photographers

Bob Calmer
John Hetherington
Hopkins Associates
William Hopkins
Jim Kascoutas

Illustrators

Jamie Downing
Kim Downing
Mike Henry
Lippisch Design Inc.
Ode Designs
Carson Ode
Greg Roberts
Jim Stevenson
Bill Zaun

If you would like to order any additional copies of our books, call 1-800-678-2802 or check with your local bookstore.